'LOOKING BACK'
at
CANFORD CLIFFS
POOLE, DORSET

by

IRIS MORRIS

Old Thyme Publishing
2nd Floor
Jonsen House
43 Commercial Road
Poole Dorset BH14 0HU

The author has lived in Poole for over 40 years,
and has published three other local history books -

1993 The Llewellin Family of Upton House

1996 'Looking Back'
A Social History of the Village of Ashley Cross in Parkstone

1999 'Looking Back' at Lilliput

©Iris Morris 2001
All rights reserved

ISBN 0 9520752 3 7

Every care has been taken to make this book as accurate
and comprehensive as possible, but the publishers
cannot accept responsibility for errors and omissions.

No reproduction of this book in whole or in part is
allowed except with the written permission of the publishers.

Cover photographs courtesy of:
Front cover - painting of Canford Cliffs Library by Barbara Greensmith
Back cover - postcards Mr Lewis Shaw
hand coloured photograph of 'Braidley' Mr Ronald Pratt
Inside covers - Canford Cliffs Land Society

Designed and printed by Marquee Print (01202) 769077
www.marqueeprint.com

CONTENTS

Chapter One	In The Beginning	4
Chapter Two	Western Road - The Library - Martello Park	8
Chapter Three	Village Hall - Post Office	12
Chapter Four	Canford Cliffs Hotel - The Esplanade - Maxwell Road	16
Chapter Five	Village Shops - Telephone Exchange	21
Chapter Six	Redmoor School - The Fitz Club - The Sea Witch Hotel	33
Chapter Seven	The Cliff Drive - St. Clair Road - Haven Road - Imbrecourt	37
Chapter Eight	Canford Cliffs Road - Compton Acres - Forsyte Shades	47
Chapter Nine	Nairn Road - St. Ann's Hospital - Reverend Brian Hession	53
Chapter Ten	Harbour Heights Hotel - The Conning Towers	58
Chapter Eleven	Havenhurst Hotel - Chaddesley Glen - Little Fosters	62
Chapter Twelve	Chines - Promenade - Simpson's Folly	68
Chapter Thirteen	Church of The Transfiguration	72
	Appendix 'A'	84
	Acknowledgements and Bibliography	89
	Index	90

CHAPTER ONE
IN THE BEGINNING

Originally part of the vast Canford Manor Estate, which was mentioned in the Domesday Book of 1086, Canford Cliffs (or Canford Lawns) would have once only been familiar to smugglers and the men of the Preventive Service. Canford Cliffs as an area was made part of Poole, with Sandbanks, under the Boundary Act of 1832 and three years later came into the Poole Authority for municipal purposes.

Land on the 'Canford Cliffs Estate, West Bournemouth' began to be sold as freehold building plots in the 1880s, and covered the area from Flaghead Chine in the west, Spencer Road to the north and Ravine Road to the east. Land to the west of the Estate belonged to Baron Wimborne and that to the east was marked the 'Branksome Estate'.

In the original Conditions of Sale, Stipulations as to Title mention the Canford Enclosure Act of 1805 and a Map of the Canford Award dated 1822. An Indenture of Conveyance of 10th December 1861 gives the names - The Right Honourable Charles Frederick Ashley Cooper, Lord de Mauley and the Earl of Bessborough, together with Jane Jeffrey, Sarah Hunt, Samuel Solly and R.H. Parr (these last two appear on documents relating to land at Lilliput and Ashley Cross).

John Joshua Jebb and George Samuel William Jebb, both of Boston in Lincolnshire, together with Gerald Francis Ellison of Warwick Square in London, a Lieutenant-Colonel in His Majesty's Army, are noted in a document relating to the Land Transfer Acts of 1875 and 1897 in connection with 'Freehold Land, part of the Canford Cliffs Estate near Bournemouth situate in the Parish of Parkstone in the County of Dorset'.

In October 1889 when Messrs Harman Brothers held an auction in a marquee on the Estate, the only properties marked on their plan were 'Carkeel' (now Norfolk Lodge Hotel), 'St. Hilaire' (once a school, then The Fitz Club and now an apartment block 'Haven Heights') 'Morwinstow' in Haven Road, which served as the Estate Office in 1886, run by Mr Frank Holloway, and the Post Office in Ravine Road opposite what is now a car park.

Approximately thirty plots had already been sold, and in many instances the vendors were Charles Robert Hutchings (a Bournemouth solicitor), George James Piercy, Reginald George Pinder, Samuel Edward Kemp-Welch and Thomas Bodley Scott. The latter was a Trustee of the Estate and Bodley Road was named after him - St. Clair, Beaumont and Langdown Roads were similarly named after other Trustees, although Langdown was later changed to MacAndrew Road - after a Mrs MacAndrew who was a Poole Councillor.

Prior to the 1889 Auction by Harman Brothers, it appears that several Ballots were held between January 1886 and September 1887 at The Bijou Hall in Albert Road, Bournemouth. The solicitors were Piercy and Hutchings and the architects Kemp-Welch and Pinder, all of Bournemouth. The Ballot Notices contained the following information:- 'Carriages will be provided to convey persons who wish to view the Estate leaving Albert Road at 11.00 am'. Plot 41 was sold on 22nd October 1886 for the sum of £310.00; this is believed to refer to the site on which now stands The Sea Witch Hotel in Haven Road by the roundabout.

Although Harman Brothers of Aldermanbury, in London, held many of the auctions on the Canford Cliffs Estate (sometimes in conjunction with Rebbeck Brothers of Gervis Place, Bournemouth) other surveyors, land agents, architects and auctioneers were involved - F.G. Wheatley and Son with H.E. Hawker and Mitchell of St. Peter's Chambers in Bournemouth, Messrs Segrave, Browett and Taylor of High Holborn, Messrs Thomas and Bettridge of Birmingham, Messrs Philip and George Geen of London and Messrs Pinder and Fogerty of St. Peter's Terrace, Bournemouth. The Auctions took place at '3 o'clock precisely' in a marquee, and in some cases luncheon was served at 2 o'clock.

Special trains from London and Birmingham were available and 'Cheap Railway Tickets and Luncheon Tickets may be had of the Auctioneers'. In 1898 London buyers could leave Waterloo at 9.30 am and return from Bournemouth West Station at 6.28 pm at a cost of 5s.0d.(.25p). Those from Birmingham would leave on the day of the sale at 7.28 am and return by train the next day at a cost of 8s.0d.(.40p).

The Canford Cliffs Estate was described on the auction particulars as *'charmingly situated on the west side of Bournemouth, stretching some 2000 feet along the coastline and having an almost due south aspect, with a gentle slope towards the sea. Elevated 120 feet above sea level on dry gravel and sand sub-soil, it occupies a large tract of moorland, studded with pines, which rise in stately grandeur down to the very edge of the rugged cliffs. As a sheltered position this estate is probably unique; the dense woods of Branksome protect it from the north and east winds, while the Purbeck Hills ward off the westerly gales'*.

The necessary information regarding sewers is mentioned, and 'exceedingly pure water is supplied from the waterworks near at hand, and 6 inch and 9 inch water mains are laid in the principal roads. The Post and Telegraph Office is in full working order'.

Words of persuasion directed at prospective buyers pointed out that 'residences are being erected in all directions and building land is eagerly sought after at high prices. This auction, therefore, not only presents an unusually good opportunity for purchasing Freehold Sites for the immediate erection of Marine Residences in one of the healthiest and choicest spots on the south coast, but also offers an excellent opportunity for acquiring Safe and Improving Freehold Land Investments'.

Other attractions of the area were listed - beautiful pleasure and lawn tennis grounds, fine sandy beaches, bathing and boating, anchorage for yachts, excellent fishing (bass, pout, mullet) and capital wildfowl shooting. Walks in all directions were suggested - Branksome Pine Woods, the sea-shore, neighbouring moorland, the sandbanks which bound Poole Harbour, and 'the approach from the railway station via The Avenue and Western Road is the Prettiest Walk in the neighbourhood'.

Information relating to transport indicated that negotiations were in progress to extend the Tramway System to Branksome Park, Canford Cliffs and Sandbanks; the London and South Western Railway Company were 'leaving no stone unturned' to improve the facilities for travelling between Bournemouth and London, Pullman Cars would soon be in use and the journey would shortly be accomplished within $2\frac{1}{2}$ hours. Branksome Junction Station is within easy distance, and Bournemouth West is not much further.

It was stipulated that the value of the proposed detached properties must not be less than either £600.00 or £750.00. For some strange reason, it was stated that Plot 127 on The Esplanade should contain semi-detached residences. Lot 39 was sold to Mr Hugh C. Godfray of Finsbury Pavement, in the City of London, on 29th August 1895 for the sum of £415.00. It was described as having lovely sea views, overlooking the Chine and having a frontage of 50 feet to Beaumont Road, 104 feet to Bodley Road and a return frontage of 197 feet to Cliff Drive.

Among other sites available at that same auction in 1895 were three large plots in Spencer Road, all of which were 200 feet in depth and with wide frontages; the Particulars described them as 'specially noticeable for their sunny and sheltered position and the uncommonly good views of the Isle of Wight over the Branksome Woods'. How the trees must have grown. A valuable corner site on Beaumont Road was for sale and two 'beautiful' plots in Ravine Road, as well as the parcel of land on which the Canford Cliffs Hotel was eventually built.

In Haven Road, which Poole Corporation had agreed to take over as a Highway, were four plots, eight plots in Flaghead Road and seven on Cliff Drive - five of which had 'absolute and indefeasible command of the Magnificent view of the whole sweep of the Bay'. There were nine sites on The Esplanade 'commanding specially lovely sea views over the Pleasure Grounds and the mouth of the Ravine. These views can never be built out'.

Ten shop sites were for sale in The Arcade. This, in fact, is Maxwell Road and it was originally envisaged that both sides of the road would contain shops and that there would be an 'accommodation road' at the back. It was also proposed that The Arcade (Maxwell Road) would continue straight across Haven Road, thus creating cross roads in the centre of the village.

The first row of shops to be built in Haven Road was on the south side between Ravine Road and Maxwell Road - known as Grand Parade, the date of 1909 can be seen above Rawlings. It is believed that these premises may once have been a gift shop which had a monkey in the backyard. In 1905 there were a number of shop sites available on the north side of Haven Road - this was known as The Parade and is remembered by some as originally a sandpit. The auctioneers suggested that these plots offered excellent openings on the Estate for the following trades - chemist, grocer, builder and decorator, dairyman, greengrocer, fishmonger, draper or bootmaker.

To Gentlemen requiring a Marine Residence, Architects, Builders, Investors and Speculators.

BOURNEMOUTH.

The Canford Cliffs Estate,

Within an easy distance of Branksome Junction Station and Bournemouth West Station.

Illustrated Particulars, Plan and Conditions of Sale,

OF 43 EXCEEDINGLY CHOICE AND VALUABLE

FREEHOLD

BUILDING PLOTS

With Excellent Frontages and considerable depths and Ripe for the immediate erection of

GOOD MARINE RESIDENCES,

AND

A FEW SHOPS,

ALSO A

Magnificent Hotel Site

1895. Courtesy of Canford Cliffs Land Society

CHAPTER TWO
WESTERN ROAD – THE LIBRARY – MARTELLO PARK

In the early 1900s, and until Pinecliff Road was constructed, the 'Main Road' to Westbourne was Western Road passing All Saints' Church; the only access to Branksome Chine was through Beach Road.

The junction of Haven/Western/Pinecliff Roads seems to provide a gateway into Canford Cliffs, and on the northern corner, where now stand two large apartment blocks, was once the Branksome Court Hotel. Demolished around 1970, an advertisement in the 1949-50 Poole Guide describes it as 'The Hotel in its own Estate' with seven acres of lovely grounds and on a main bus route. The telephone number was Canford Cliffs 1234. Originally built as a residence 'Westlands' for the Fisher family, there was a staircase in one corner of the library, if Mr Fisher felt disinclined to meet visitors he used the staircase as an escape route. When it became an hotel (date unknown) the library was used as the dining room. Miss Helen Brotherton CBE, whose family moved to Martello Park in 1946, remembers the Branksome Court as a well-run establishment under the ownership of Mr T Woolf. Her parents and their guests were regular patrons and held their own house warming party at the hotel. A 1965 RAC Handbook tells us that there were 50 bedrooms (32 en-suite) and that the daily tariff was 59s.6d - 77s.6d (£2.97p - £3.87p) and dinner 15s.0d (.75p).

Cliff Café and Tea Gardens, now Canford Cliffs Library
Courtesy: Mr Lewis Shaw

On the opposite side of the road is Canford Cliffs Library which, on Thursday 19th October 2000 held an Open Day attended by the Mayor of Poole Councillor Joyce Jones, to celebrate the library's half century.

Originating as the lodge to 'Westlands' (Branksome Court) the building was described by Pevsner as 'rough cast with arched window recesses and segment-headed dormers' designed by J H Brewerton and built around 1913, with a similar cottage to the rear. In due time the property became the Cliff Café, owned and controlled by the Parks Committee, and there are many folk who remember it as a delightful and popular café with tables and chairs in the garden during the summer. Listed in the 1939 Kelly's Directory is the manager Walter Vinecombe Cornish and he lived in the Cliff Café Lodge.

The residents of Canford Cliffs had wanted a library of their own for some time but difficulty had been experienced in finding a suitable site. However at the Libraries Committee meeting in January 1945 plans were approved by the Borough Engineer to adapt a portion of the ground floor of the Cliff Café as a branch library; the estimated cost of conversion being £500.00.

It was not until 12th October 1950 that the new library was opened by the Sheriff of Poole, Miss M M Llewellin, Chairman of the Public Libraries Committee. A number of local dignitaries were present including Alderman A B Haynes, Deputy Mayor and Vice-Chairman of the Parks Committee and Mr B C Short, who had been Borough Librarian for 46 years. A newspaper report of the time described it as probably one of the most picturesque in the country *'set amid towering pine trees just off the main road on the Bournemouth side of Canford Cliffs Village, the new library boasts a small but pretty garden complete with lily-covered goldfish pond, crazy paths and a lawn with artificial toad-stools'*. The interior was decorated in light and dark cream and was equipped to hold 8000 books, although at the opening there were only 3000 on the metal book shelves well lit by strip lamps.

There have been four head librarians - Doreen Newman 1950 - 1959, Dawn Prattley 1959 - 1989, Sally Sharpley 1989 - 1999 and Ann Elger 1999 - 2001. They all attended the Centenary Open Day on 19th October 2000, and many memories were exchanged with readers and ex-library assistants.

Doreen Newman recalls that business was slow at first with residents taking a little while to appreciate the useful facility on their doorstep. One comment seems to have been 'what an extraordinary place to put a library, who will use it?' Dawn Prattley remembers the fumes from the gas fires in winter, and the many amusing incidents involving borrowers struggling to open the gate that was then in place and which was foot-operated by brass pedals inside the desk.

The weather caused problems over the years - during the drought in the summer of 1979 the building was almost surrounded by scorched bushes, a huge tree fell across the front of the library during the night of 24th January 1990, and although very little damage was done, everyone had to use the back door for a day or two. A severe winter meant closing early on one occasion, and assistance given to a couple of hardy readers to get them home safely. One assistant recalls the library being used as an occasional trysting-place by a mature couple who, if one failed to arrive, would wait disconsolately for half an hour before reluctantly going home.

A reader, who has been using the library for nearly 50 years is appreciative *'of our very own library in Canford Cliffs, where once my children chose their books in front of a coal fire and where now my grandchildren enjoy the Internet'*.

In this year of 2001, residents have the choice of 11,000 titles with access to the Internet and audio-visual material; 'The Friends of Canford Cliffs Library' was launched in the Spring of 2001. The first floor of the library is in use as the offices of the Poole Maritime Trust.

Playing its part in the community of Canford Cliffs, the library has always had a happy and friendly atmosphere, and this is being sustained by the present assistants, Val Short and Carol Burbidge, under the guiding hand of the new Library Manager Mr David Hinton.

Martello Park lies on the cliff top to the west of the library and now contains a number of apartment blocks, many of which are named after the original houses built there in the 1930s - Stanton Lacy, Sandbourne, Owlshott, South Lodge, Leyton Conyers, Burnage House, Burnage Cottage and Treetops.

This postcard of 1948 presents an aerial view of Martello Park showing a number of private tennis courts in the gardens and the various footpaths leading down the cliff-side. Courtesy: Mr Lewis Shaw

When Miss Helen Brotherton CBE and her parents went to live in Burnage House in 1946 there was a croquet lawn and a footpath leading down to the beach, on which the wartime defences were still in place. These had caused shallow water to form on the seaward side and attracted many and various sea birds. At that time, Poole Borough Council wanted to buy their stretch of beach below Burnage House for cliff protection works, but it later transpired that they really wanted it in order to extend the promenade.

Miss Brotherton, who has been President of the Dorset Wildlife Trust for many years, remembers that the Canford Cliffs area was a haven for wildlife in the days after WWII; the footpaths on top of the cliffs were overgrown (as was the library garden) and this attracted birds and animals including red and grey squirrels. Foxes were a rarity then (unlike now) and most gardens had sand lizards. At the time when the chemical DDT was diminishing sparrow-hawks elsewhere in the country, the wood opposite the library (now the large car park) held one of the very few pairs which raised young in a particular year.

Apart from her active work for the Dorset Wildlife Trust, Miss Brotherton has given many years of service to the National Trust. Together with Mr Leslie Miller she formed the Brownsea Island Preservation Committee in 1961 after the death of the last private owner of the Island, Mrs Florence Bonham-Christie. The Committee was responsible for raising the endowment sum of £100,000.00, thus ensuring that Brownsea Island was saved for the Nation to be cared for by The National Trust.

Travelling towards the shops, still in Western Road, 'Westhaven' is on the north corner with Ravine Road. Although the Estate Plan of 1889 indicates that the plot had then been sold, the 1918 Kelly's Directory does not show a property on the site. However, by 1939 we know that it was called 'The Dorset Corner House Private Hotel' run by Harry and Mrs Primmer, and an advertisement in the 1949/50 Poole Guide tells us that Mrs May Tait was then proprietress. It has been suggested that 'Westhaven' was once owned by Admiral de Horsey and that it might have been a Club, pre-dating The Fitz Club in Haven Road.

By 1961 the property had been converted into five flats with F R Wilde MD LRCP Physician and Surgeon occupying Flat One. Dr Wilde, at one stage, ran his private practice from Haig Avenue, and is still remembered by a number of Canford Cliffs residents. 'Westhaven' is still in use as flats.

CHAPTER THREE
VILLAGE HALL - POST OFFICE

Canford Cliffs Village 1922, facing west - Voysey's the bakers on left
Courtesy: Mr Lewis Shaw

Turning right into Ravine Road the Village Hall is to be found a few yards on the left, on the corner of Moorfields Road; built in 1923, it is now experiencing a revival of interest in the area after being in the doldrums for a few years.

A document dated 29th September 1923 is headed 'Hall and Institute' and is described as a Declaration of Trust. The names of the five Trustees were: Sir John Archer of Devonshire Lodge Richmond in the County of Surrey a Knight Commander of the Most Excellent Order of the British Empire, Edward Hewitt of The Plateau Canford Cliffs in the County of Dorset Esquire, Samuel Hage Titley of Westhome Canford Cliffs aforesaid Esquire, Wilfred Eustace Milne-Redhead of Thurnham Canford Cliffs aforesaid Esquire, and Edith Rudd of Redmoor Canford Cliffs aforesaid Spinster.

The document states *'We are the registered proprietors with absolute title under the Land Transfer Acts 1875 and 1879 of all that plot of land situate at Canford Cliffs in the County of Dorset formerly forming part of the Canford Cliffs Estate.....and Whereas certain buildings have recently been erected on the said land to the intent that the same shall be used as a Hall and Institute (with a residence for caretakers). The buildings shall be used for the education, recreation and otherwise for the advantage and benefit of the inhabitants residing in and persons visiting Canford Cliffs and the adjoining part of the Borough of Poole and the adjoining Borough of Bournemouth'.*

'The buildings shall not be used exclusively for the purpose of any particular church, religious body or political party nor for any organisation formed for the furtherance of any particular religious, political, social, scientific, philanthropic or other object. The buildings shall be managed by a Committee to be from time to time appointed by the Trustees and that they may from time to time make rules and regulations as to the manner in which the Committee shall manage the buildings. All monies received by way of rent in connection with the letting of the said buildings shall be applied for insurance, rates, taxes, repairs and renewals and for the wages of anyone employed for these purposes'.

If at any time the Trustees considered the Hall and Institute to be inconveniently situated and might benefit from a different site they were empowered to sell the land and the buildings and use the proceeds to purchase another site and erect equip and endow a new Hall and Institute.

One of the original Committee members, who worked closely with Sir Leonard Lyle, was Mr William George; coming from the Midlands he built a house in Spencer Road in 1921 and became involved with many of the local activities. He was a member of the Canford Cliffs Land Society, Warden at the Church of the Transfiguration, secretary of the Canford Cliffs Tennis Club in Lilliput Road, was on the Flower Show Committee and served in the Royal Observer Corps during WWII (the Observation Post was on the top of the cliffs). He is also believed to have been the first Canford Cliffs resident to own a motor car.

His daughter, Mrs Eileen Greenhill has lived in the area all her life - their house in Spencer Road had a path through to Newton Road for their own use, making a short cut to the village shops. Mrs Greenhill played badminton in the village hall before WWII and went on to represent England in that sport. In the Ambulance Service during the war she remembers sleeping one night alone in the hall, where some of their equipment was stored.

In its early years, the hall was the venue for a variety of activities - regular sessions of badminton and bridge, seasonal flower shows and annual dances. The Canford Cliffs Mens' Club met in the room under the hall to play snooker, and still in existence is 'The Huntsmans Cup for Snooker' presented by Messrs Eldridge Pope and Company Limited in February 1936 - these are the names engraved on the base:

1936 E C Eames	1948 P Pickering
1937 R B Barrett	1949 C Pratt
1938 J H Rice	1950 E C Ames
1939 R B Barrett	1951 K H Robinson
1945 E C Ames	1952 H Fletcher
1947 H Bolden	

Another trophy still existing is one representing prize delphiniums grown by Mr Mark (aka Charles) Pratt, who came to Canford Cliffs in 1911 as gardener to the Misses Darroch on Cliff Drive. The inscription is "SEDHS" - the South East Dorset Horticultural Society - 1935. This Society was known for the splendid Flower Shows held in August at the Old Ride School in Martello Road. Mr Pratt's son, Ronald, remembers helping Mr William George with the stands in the marquees; the owners of the large houses basked in the glory of winning and their gardeners received the prizes. This Flower Show was apparently a great event - those at the village hall were small spring and autumn ones by comparison.

The Canford Cliffs Women's Institute was started in 1925 at the village hall, and during the 1960s the meetings are remembered as being very lively with a membership of 140 (young Ronald Pratt recalls attending some of the meetings with his mother). The opening of the Lilliput Women's Institute in 1969 halved the membership of Canford Cliffs and was further depleted when another one opened in Westbourne. Their records were stored in a member's garage during WWII, and subsequently destroyed by fire. Still very active, the thirty two current members of the Canford Cliffs Women's Institute now meet, for reasons of economy, at St. Joseph's Church Hall on Bournemouth Road. Whilst clearing out the roof space of the village hall recently, Mr Maurice Shutler, the present caretaker, found an old clock in pieces; this has now been restored by him and hangs on a wall - it was made in Bournemouth and was presented to the village hall in 1933 by the Canford Cliffs Women's Institute.

Until a short time ago very few organisations used the village hall, but there are now plenty of activities for residents to enjoy. Regular sessions of Keep Fit (for the elderly), childrens dancing classes, U3A (University of the Third Age), badminton, Kung-fu, line dancing and free coffee mornings run by the Retired and Senior Voluntary Programme (RSVP) where help and advice is available on various subjects. As well as Annual General Meetings of local organisations, childrens parties and discos are held, and also the monthly Saturday Market and Fair.

Returning to cross the Haven Road junction into the southern part of Ravine Road, the car park is on the left; this was once a Corporation taxi rank where Fred Pethen kept his vehicles for hire. The original plot was an extensive one, occupying approximately half an acre, with a frontage to Ravine Road of 140 feet and to the main road 180 feet. It was for sale in 1890 and eventually a large house 'Kingsland' was built close to the Canford Cliffs Hotel with the garden down to the main road. Remembered by many folk, Mr & Mrs E Lionel Blake and their daughter lived there for many years.

Opposite, in 1918, was the Canford Cliffs Motor Omnibuses Depot, found along the service road behind the Grand Parade shops, and A D Greenwood, grocer, occupied the premises where Guy Pound Architects used to be (now used by Careline Telemarketing). It has been confusing tracking down the whereabouts of the Canford Cliffs Post Office and Telegraph Office. Archives state that it opened on 1st April 1890, under Parkstone, as a rural office, was transferred to Bournemouth on 1st April 1891, became a sub-office to Bournemouth on 1st April 1893 and was re-located as a town sub-office, under Poole, on 26th April 1962.

The site plan of 1889 shows the position of the Post Office to be in the premises of A D Greenwood, as above, but by 1903 it had moved to the corner of Ravine Road with Levi George Cosh (refreshment rooms, sweets, stationery, tobacconists and Post Office), and an old postcard exists showing the shop. In 1915 the actual address changed from Ravine to Haven Road but the property stayed in the same place. However, it was run by Mrs B M Dean in 1918/1920 on the north side of Haven Road between The Tobacco Stores and Lowe Brothers Motor Engineers, and then moved back across the road to Grand Parade (south side) between Ravine and Maxwell Roads. Mr A D Greenwood would appear to have still been in business in 1927/1928 because he is listed as sub-postmaster in his grocer's shop in Ravine/Haven Road, and still there in 1939. By 1957 the Canford Cliffs Post Office seemed to have found a permanent home as it was in the Chemist's shop run by Mr S Short on the corner of Haven Road with Elmstead Road. Later, this was Penny's Perfumery and the Post Office is still there within the Haven Road News at number 46.

Motor Car Station at Canford Cliffs Village c 1900
Courtesy: Canford Cliffs Land Society

CHAPTER FOUR
CANFORD CLIFFS HOTEL – THE ESPLANADE MAXWELL ROAD

On Saturday 20th September 1890 Harman Brothers of Aldermanbury, Guildhall in London, in conjunction with Rebbeck Brothers of Gervis Place, Bournemouth held the auction of 'a magnificent hotel site' on the Canford Cliffs Estate. Taking place in a marquee it was timed for 'Three o'Clock Precisely'. Should you have been travelling from London you might have availed yourself of a Special Train which left Waterloo Station at 9.35am calling at Clapham Junction and Basingstoke, and returning in the evening, the cost of which was 5s.0d (25p) return.

The auction particulars stipulated that any building erected on the plot (over an acre) could not be used for trade, manufacture or business other than a first-class hotel or similar establishment, that the property could not be of less value than £2,500 and the Vendors reserved the right to cut back the face of the cliff fifty feet from the existing edge.

We do not know how many potential buyers attended the auction, but the site did not sell on that occasion and was auctioned again in 1895. We do know that by 1905 the Canford Cliffs Hotel had been built and was open for business. Situated on the cliff top at the end of Ravine Road, it had splendid sea views with a four hundred foot frontage to the 21 acres of Canford Cliffs Pleasure Grounds which included a chine, cliff top and tennis courts.

According to Tony Crouch, who lived above his grandfather's shop in Canford Cliffs as a child, the hotel was indeed very exclusive, visited by foreign Royalty and Heads of State, who came with their chauffeurs, nannies, maids and valets. The chauffeurs had their own quarters in the grounds and the other servants were lodged in nearby houses.

Canford Cliffs Hotel 1911
Courtesy: Mr Lewis Shaw.

The hotel owned a stretched Austin which was used to transport guests to and from the railway station; eventually the car ended its days as a taxi in the hands of Thornes Garage in Canford Cliffs Village. Many guests arrived in their own cars, but if not a Rolls-Royce, the staff would call these visitors by the name of their vehicles - i.e. Ford or Austin - perhaps an inverted form of snobbery.

With a large kitchen garden, the hotel unusually owned its own electricity generating station - this was even before the Village itself was electrified. It seems that part of the Canford Cliffs promenade was owned by the hotel and still to be seen is a spot where the design of the wall changes. A zig-zag path led down the cliff and on summer days waiters could be seen nipping up and down carrying tea trays aloft for the happy guests on the beach.

All this changed when on 10th April 1941, nineteen months after the outbreak of World War II, the Canford Cliffs Hotel was partially destroyed by enemy action. On that April night many incendiary bombs landed in the Poole and Parkstone area, and demand was so great for water to douse the burning buildings that there was nothing left in the mains supply. The fire at the hotel was, therefore, left to burn itself out; some paintings were rescued and a few lucky looters found an area littered with intact champagne bottles. The next day the Royal Engineers Bomb Disposal Unit found and de-fused eight unexploded bombs in Haven Road, giving a lucky escape to many residents.

Dick Hartley lived in Elmstead Road as a lad and clearly remembers that night - some of the bombs fell in the woods around their house, one fell at the top of Cliff Drive, near the shops, killing Dr Bartholomew Langran and his grandson at 'Balcormo' and another fell in Newton Road destroying one house. After these incidents Dick Hartley saw a glow to the south and set out to investigate - he had a spectacular view of the Canford Cliffs Hotel burning to the ground.

A few of the hotel buildings remained after the fire, and the four flats above the garages in the chauffeurs quarters were subsequently used by BOAC personnel. Eventually, once the war ended, the brewers, Strong and Company, acquired the building and it was converted into the only 'pub' in Canford Cliffs. At one stage it was owned by the late Councillor Freddie Rowe, former Mayor and ex-Sheriff of Poole.

The heyday of the Canford Cliffs Hotel, as it continued to be called, was the period from 1954 to 1975 when Mr & Mrs Jimmy Cooper were the well known licensees. The conversion of the old chauffeurs' quarters was designed by architects, A J Seal, whose name is found in connection with many buildings in the area.

Mrs Jean Cooper, who now lives in Parkstone, was responsible for the interior design and furnishings of the two bars, and has many memories of those years. The catering side of the 'pub' proved very popular and it was visited late one night by Egon Ronay. Not much food was available but apparently his meal of home-made soup, lemon sole, cheese and coffee was sufficient for him to recommend the Canford Cliffs Hotel for a star, and a glowing report later appeared in the Bournemouth Echo.

Poole Teachers' Tennis Tournament at the Canford Cliffs Hotel 1960s
Sid James presents prizes. Courtesy: Mrs Jean Cooper

The two hard tennis courts in the grounds were used by local people and Wednesday afternoons were reserved for a Parkstone Girls School. Tournaments were held between local clubs, and here is a photograph of the late Sid James presenting the prizes.

Jimmy Cooper was a golfing enthusiast which brought him into contact with Showbiz Personalities who played at Parkstone Golf Club, and the Canford Cliffs Hotel became a favourite haunt for a considerable number of them - Eric Sykes, Roy Castle, Dickie Henderson, Eric Morecombe, Bruce Forsyth, Dick Emery, Max Bygraves - to name but a few. The atmosphere created by the licensees enabled the entertainers to relax without fear of being pestered by autograph hunters.

The brewery decided to close the Canford Cliffs Hotel in August 1975, and at the age of 66, Jimmy Cooper bowed out of the licensed trade. In previous years he had worked at the Royal Bath, Exeter and Burlington Hotels, was manager of The Fitz Club in 1949 and before coming to the Canford Cliffs Hotel, was at the Anchor and Hope in Lymington. Headlines in the local paper at that time included 'Stars Favourite Haunt Will Go Into Eclipse' and 'No Reprieve for the Stars Pub'.

As a surprise parting gift for the 'redundant landlord' the entertainers who had become accustomed to visiting the Canford Cliffs Hotel, clubbed together and gave Jimmy Cooper a set of golf clubs as a 'thank you' for making them welcome over the years.

Although in August 1975 it seemed likely that the Canford Cliffs Hotel would remain closed, negotiations took place between the interested parties and it re-opened in the September, under management. It is now run by Bass as 'The Night Jar'.

The Canford Cliffs Hotel had the benefit of a considerable frontage to the 21 acres of the Pleasure Grounds, and it must be assumed that The Esplanade was so named because sea views were then apparent, and it had been intended that the north eastern corner of the Grounds would contain a Bandstand. On the north side of the Esplanade several houses were built around 1900 and the 1918 Kelly's Directory lists five houses - Marina, South View, Canford Chine, Ravine Head and towards Cliff Drive, Brampton Kinlet.

Max Bygraves and the late Jimmy Cooper, Licensee Canford Cliffs Hotel 1970s. Courtesy: Mrs Jean Cooper

None of the original house names remained by 1939, Dr Robert Stephen Risk MD BS MRCS LRCP was at 'Cartmel', and The Riviera Hotel (Mrs F Nash-Wortham, Director) had appeared. By the 1960's 'Cartmel' had become a private hotel with Mr & Mrs E L Tindle as proprietors, and was still there in 1975. The Riviera Hotel was then run by Ralph Evans Limited and their advertisement in the 1984 Poole Guide describes the establishment as 'A reasonably priced well-appointed 30 bedroom hotel with First Class Chefs and a renowned cellar'. The Bridge Room provided 'cut in' rubber bridge daily throughout the year, and the hotel gradually became known for its Bridge Holidays. In due time the establishment became entirely residential before being demolished and apartments built on the site.

Maxwell Road, as mentioned elesewhere, was originally intended to be The Arcade with rows of shops, but became a residential road. There were only six properties in 1918 - St Clare, The Homestead, Chernocke House, St Catherine's, The Pines and Lingwood. In addition there was a Fire Station, this in fact was sited along the service road behind the shops where Mr Crouch had his furniture workshops. By 1939 this had disappeared and there were twelve properties in Maxwell Road. The school run by Miss Gweneth Medwin was at The Homestead, two medical men, Dr Francis Grey Bennett and Dr William Vere Taylor Styles were at Chernocke House and the house 'Little Slam' was reputed to have been acquired with bridge earnings. More houses had been converted into flats in 1961, and The Reverend F L W Sealy was to be found at Maxwell Studios; the 1975 Kelly's Directory no longer quoted house names, but numbers only.

CHAPTER FIVE
VILLAGE SHOPS – TELEPHONE EXCHANGE

(See Appendix "A" for Kelly's Directory Lists of the village shops in 1918, 1939, 1961 and 1975 - plus current details for 2001)

Mrs Eve Eaton, who has lived in Canford Cliffs for many years, recalls that the various village shops once provided all daily needs with food shops of every kind including three greengrocers, chemists, three restaurants, jewellers, the 'oh so useful' haberdashery and wool shop, corsetière, china shop, small lending library, stationers and even a 'doggy' shop, the owner of which would shampoo your pet in your own home. Charles Harrison, who ran the fishmongers, is remembered by so many folk although the 'squeaking' noises which arose from the back of the shop where the lobsters were cooked did rather upset one or two. He was reckoned to be a good employer for though he expected his staff to work very long hours, he did pay well.

As a young lad, Mr Ronald Pratt worked as a paper boy in the mid-1930s for newsagent Jack Stimpson (now J M E Store); his father, Mark, (aka Charles) was chauffeur/gardener to the Misses Darroch. They had moved to 'Braidley' on Cliff Drive in 1911, coming from Berkhamsted, Hertfordshire and the Pratt family occupied a flat in the lodge behind the house. Until the education authorities decided that children should attend a school within their own borough, Ronald Pratt went to St. Ambrose in Robert Louis Stevenson Avenue, Westbourne, and in 1930 moved, with several of his contemporaries, to St. Aldhelm's School in Branksome - a Hants and Dorset bus worked its way up from Sandbanks collecting the children en route.

Mr Pratt knew most of the shopkeepers before he joined the Royal Air Force in 1940 (WW II), and remembers that A D Greenwood in Ravine Road would roast coffee beans to tempt more customers into his grocer's shop. His male assistant would go round on his bicycle to collect orders from the customers, and these would subsequently be delivered by a Model 'T' Ford Van. Voysey's Bakery, run by a 'Mrs S', was serviced from their Westbourne shop by Mr Willis in his van which had been converted from a Buick motor car, and Fred Pethen with his brother Billy ran the taxi rank from where is now the car park. George S Day had a bullnose Morris Van which could be converted into a two seater car with a dicky seat, and Mr William T Crouch & Sons (Robert and Frank) was in charge of the Fire Station as well as running the furniture repair business. In 1918 Greatorex & Crowe, haberdashers (they also published postcards) stood on the corner of Haven with Maxwell Road (where is now Rawlings), and the next owners, Mrs M P Smith and her daughter Barbara, drapers are well remembered by Ronald Pratt.

Before Jack Stimpson took over the newsagents on the other corner of Maxwell Road, it was called P K Chesters, and Mr Walter Hales was the manager. After the arrival of Mr Stimpson, he set up his own tobacconists and confectioners only a few yards away at number fourteen; Walter Hales did not prosper - he had hoped to obtain the Post Office franchise but it was not forthcoming. The site between this shop and St. Clair Café was once a wood owned by George Fox after he had sold his garage (later Canford Cliffs Motors) on the opposite of Haven Road, and Ronald Pratt remembers playing there with the sons of Mr Fox, whose nickname was Greasy Fox. He also recalls the mother of George Day, who moved to his 'new' shop in 1933 on the other side of the road. She was a sprightly lady and once gave the young lad a firm lecture on profit and loss with regard to the perishable commodities of fruit and vegetables.

Canford Cliffs Motors 1988
Author's Collection

The Kelly's Directories (see Appendix "A") show that on the north side of Haven Road there were, in 1939 and 1961, two garages. Where is now Magna Motors was number 19, the newsagents run by the two Parish sisters, (whose brother was manager of Richard Godsell, Estate Agents, at Number 35) and Miss Jane Mann, corsetière, then at numbers 20 and 21 was Canford Cliffs Motors with a shop front and a wide open gangway through the building to workshops behind the Canford Cliffs Fruit Stores run by Jack Channell and his sister. A few doors away was Thornes Garage run by Frank Thorne and his son George; petrol was served across the pavement and Mrs Thorne sat inside the shop awaiting the next customer. As well as the usual garage facilities, they provided cars for hire and had a large workshop which faced on to the service lane at the rear - this is now Hamilton Motors. Thornes Garage was still in existence in 1961 but had disappeared by 1975. In addition to their presence at numbers 20 and 21, Canford Cliffs Motors in 1961, ran the petrol service station on the corner with Ravine Road (this was once a wooded area) and by 1975 they were also agents for Renault Cars. Still with motor vehicles, Robert B Barrett & Son at number 29 ran a Rolls Royce hire car service and on Saturdays Mr Barrett often took a party of local supporters to the football match in Boscombe.

As a 'Saturday Boy' Ronald Pratt worked for the ironmongers Scott & Scott at number 23; this was run by a Mr Ernie Eldridge, who imparted many useful skills of the trade to the young lad. Stationed just along this stretch of shops, possibly down the alleyway to the service road, in 1939, was a young Police Constable and his wife. Prior to this date, cover was from the Police House in Bingham Avenue, and Constables remembered are Summers, Travers, and Fish.

A reputable builder of many Canford Cliffs properties was Mr Henry Joseph Hillman; his office was more or less where Canford Aviation is now, and he lived at 'Delina' in Moorfields Road, in which six houses were listed in 1939. His yard, two storey workshop and lorry garage were at the rear of the premises - many and various workshops were to be found in this service road, up to and including the land adjacent to the village hall. Mr Hillman built the house on Furzey Island for Lord and Lady Iliffe as well as the property on Round Island. Some of this building work took place during the school summer holidays for Mr Hillman's son, Dennis and Ronald Pratt were allowed to go across in the open launch when Mr Hillman went over to supervise the work in progress - the lads spent their days fishing (apparently more successfully off Furzey than Round Island) but were not permitted to land.

At number 36, next to Mr Short, the chemist, a Greek couple, Mr and Mrs A Alborno, ran the first shop in Canford Cliffs to sell cooked meat, and their hot potato crisps were remembered with pleasure.

Before joining the Royal Air Force in 1940 Ronald Pratt remembers that the first property to be burnt out during the war was 'Whiteley Wood', a bungalow on the corner of Flaghead Road and Cliff Drive. Firemen carried out a sideboard with a whisky bottle on top and when this fell off and broke, there was a sympathetic cheer from the onlookers. The garage at the Norfolk Lodge Hotel was damaged by an incendiary bomb and Ronald Pratt helped to push the cars to safety.

Now living in Bear Wood, Mr Pratt's memories of the years prior to 1939 are of an 'upstairs downstairs' atmosphere, but do paint a picture of a pleasant, slow pace of life where the residents and the shopkeepers together formed a community. Houses were rented out for the summer and sometimes these families, in order to avoid paying the local trader's bills, would vanish a few days before the appointed date. However, when residents saw removal vans at any of these premises they would advise the shopkeepers who would then hasten to collect their money.

Ronald Pratt was christened at The Church of the Transfiguration and married there in the early 1940s, and was in the choir when the new chapel of St. Nicolas on Sandbanks was dedicated.

Making the most of his new premises in 1910 at number 7 Grand Parade, Haven Road (south side) a cabinet maker, W T Crouch also ran the Fire Station with a hose reel hanging on the wall at the front of his shop, and was the local undertaker with a mortuary at the rear. His grandson, Tony Crouch, now residing in Branksome Park, lived above this shop for a while before moving across the road to number 23 The Parade (where is now Henry's Wine Bar), and later to St. Clair Road where his mother ran the Ebdon House Hotel. He remembers an Air Raid Precautions (ARP) Command Centre in the village during WWII, probably in Mr Hillman's old office, and feels certain that at the beginning of the war residents used the vault of what was then the National Provincial Bank as an air-raid shelter. One of the shops was a 'Save for Victory' Centre, and Molly St. Clair gave her name to the café on the Cliff Drive corner after Mrs M Davie retired. Apparently horses kept in Maxwell Road were used for hauling beach huts up from the Chine at the end of each summer.

Dick Hartley's memories of the area go back to 1926 when his family moved from Devon to live on the corner of Elmstead and Chaucer Roads. His father was a doctor and had actually started his Canford Cliffs practice in 1911 from a house in Flaghead Road, now called 'Ormonde'. On their return to the village they rented 'Firlands' in Canford Crescent whilst alterations were made to the Elmstead Road house which overlooked the playing fields of the Redmoor Girls School.

In the late 1920s, the Grand Parade shops ended on the east side of Maxwell Road (where is now Rawlings), and those on the north (The Parade or Jubilee Parade) at Lloyds Bank. The rest of that row, built in 1933, included two single-storey shops with a flat roof and it was not until probably the 1980s that the owners of Brown's Gift Shop built another storey on top. Prior to 1933 a footpath ran diagonally across the open space where the last shops were erected.

Dick Hartley recalls that life as a boy in Canford Cliffs prior to WWII (1939) was very pleasant, the only 'made-up' roads were Haven and Western whilst cars were a comparative rarity - his father maintained that their own should be used solely for 'motor-runs'. Great reliance was put on public transport; there were buses every fifteen minutes into Bournemouth

Canford Cliffs Village looking east 1920s. Greatorex & Crowe, haberdashers and postcard publishers, on right
Courtesy: Classic Pictures, Christchurch

or down to Sandbanks, the Gondolier motor boats ran a regular service from Wareham to Swanage calling at Poole, Sandbanks and Studland, and the paddle steamers provided a comprehensive service to Swanage, Lulworth Cove, Southampton, Portsmouth and the Isle of Wight. Twice weekly the paddle steamer 'Balmoral' sailed from Bournemouth Pier to Cherbourg for a fare of 12s.6d.(.63p) with an increase to 15s.0d.(.75p) in 1938.

In addition to the Hants and Dorset Bus Company, there were several private bus operators including Miss Foott's Favourites and Mr Randall's Cosy Coaches - Dick Hartley had a preference for their brightly coloured vehicles which were usually of the open charabanc type. The Hants and Dorset single fare to Westbourne was three pence (1p) but because of a disagreement with Bournemouth Corporation, the additional fare to Bournemouth Square was another three pence (1p) as opposed to the one penny charged on the Bournemouth Corporation Trams. The result was that he and his friends would leave the bus at Westbourne and continue the rest of the journey by tram - this suited Dick Hartley well as he was most interested at that time in the Bournemouth Corporation Tramway system which extended from Poole to Christchurch. Some years later, following agreement between Bournemouth Corporation and the Hants and Dorset Bus Company, the fare between Canford Cliffs and Bournemouth was actually reduced to four pence (2p).

A 'modest tennis club', with two hard courts, existed just down Lilliput Road on the right, almost opposite where now is the drive leading up to 'Forsyte Shades'. A Mrs Carnelly organised matches for the youngsters, and this is remembered by a number of local residents. A footpath ran through De Mauley Road from Newton Road and was a useful short cut to Canford Cliffs Road and the tennis club. It seems that part of this land belonged to Mr Simpson of Compton Acres, and once a year it was closed to prevent it becoming a right of way. In the 1980s controversy arose regarding the footpath - it was then considered to be a public right of way, but the path no longer exists although it is just possible, from De Mauley Road, to see where it ran.

One of the first businesses to be established on Grand Parade (together with W T Crouch and Sons) was Robert Day, Florist and Fruiterer, and the premises now house the restaurant Le Chateau run by David, Lesley and Sophie Wakeham, who have a framed photograph of the old fruiterers. The terrace of shops there was built 1909/1910 and what was then number five was known as The Farm Stores run by a Mr Mortimer; he did not stay long for in 1911 Robert Day, who had eight shops in the Bournemouth area, one in Westbourne, bought the business from him for £17.00. Since there were very few residents in Canford Cliffs at that time, there was not enough trade at The Farm Stores to earn a livelihood for Mr Mortimer, who later emigrated to Australia. Mrs Christine Clarke, granddaughter of Robert Day, believes that it was her grandmother who had the idea of taking over The Farm Stores because their Westbourne branch could supply small quantities to Canford Cliffs until such time as the population increased and it could become a viable business. Initially, a Miss Read was in charge and later a Mrs Chapman, and trade gradually increased.

Canford Cliffs Village 1988 - St Clair Café - now Goadsby & Harding Estate Agents.
Author's Collection

George S Day standing in front of his shop in Grand Parade - late 1920s; he later built his own larger premises on the other side of Haven Road. Note Hants & Dorset time table.
Courtesy: Mrs Christine Clarke

Robert Day's son, George S Day (Mrs Clarke's father) took over the running of the shop in 1924 and only died quite recently at the age of 96. He had written a few pages of his autobiography and his memories provide us with an insight into those years.

He lived in Westbourne with his parents but during the summer months they would move into the flat above the Canford Cliffs shop; he notes in his diary that on a number of occasions he cycled from there to the Bournemouth School for Boys. His father's substantial customers were still supplied from the Westbourne shop, notably The Haven Hotel, first under M. Poulain and later Madame Patenotte, and also St. Ann's Hospital where Miss Palma was Matron. Sometime in 1913 George Day accompanied Mr Channell on the horse and cart which was delivering to St. Ann's, the entrance of which was marked by white painted posts for guidance at night. Leaving the main road Jack Channell allowed the young George Day to drive the horse and cart down the driveway; a hub cap caught one of the posts, half the goods were tipped on the ground and the horse bolted. Luckily Mr Channell managed to bring everything under control before they reached the goods entrance.

George Day remembers waiting with a friend for the evening papers to come out from Westbourne, by a boy on a carrier bicycle, on a particular August day - as feared by everyone war had been declared - it was 4th August 1914 (WWI).

During the days when his family were in the flat above the Canford Cliffs shop, George Day spent his evenings in the bus garage with George Fox and Bert Orchard, helping to maintain the old buses. This would have been the Canford Cliffs Motor Omnibuses' depôt situated in the service road behind Grand Parade, it was owned by George Fox who later acquired Lowes Garage on the opposite side of the road. In those early days public transport was provided by two Daimler buses (numbers 503 and 504) with bodies built by N F Milnes of Birkenhead - they had been bought second-hand from Ayrshire in Scotland, and had two foot brakes, one acting on the transmission and one on the road wheels. The final drive was by exposed pinion to internal geared ring on the inner side of each rear road wheel. George Day used to ride on the open bodied bus running from County Gates to Sandbanks, and it was his task to fill up with gas oil for 1s.6d (7p) a gallon. The engine had an open pipe sliding up at the front and another at the rear, he used to pour about half a gallon into each, ready for the ascent of West Hill (lower part of Haven Road), which the bus once climbed in third gear after an overhaul. He believed that the buses were operated by the Canford Cliffs Land Society and their agent, Frank Holloway, employed George Fox, Bert Orchard and George Randall as drivers. George Day himself, as a young lad, was once allowed to drive a bus along Grand Parade.

Canford Cliffs Village 1988. Le Chateau was, from 1911 to 1933 the fruiterers run by Mr George S Day.
Author's Collection

Above what is now Pizza Rapida is the date 1933. This is the shop at 33 Haven Road that George Day had built with a two-storey flat above, for the sum of £1799.15s.6d (£1799.77p). The architect was his cousin, Frank Day, and the builder H J Hillman (mentioned elsewhere), who also erected the butcher's section of Harrison's the fishmongers. George Day ran his Fruiterers from 1913 to 1961, having sold his father's business on the opposite side of the road. When George S Day retired he introduced the next owner to his customers by printing his business cards thus: *This business which originated as a Farm Store in 1911 and is the oldest of any description in Canford Cliffs, was taken over by my family and has been operated by me since 1924. Now after 36 years I have disposed of my interest to Mr N A T McLeod. I wish to take this opportunity of expressing my very warm thanks for all the consideration I have received in the past and hope that you may have an early opportunity of meeting my successor.* Mr McLeod continued to run the shop as a fruiterers and florists, changing its name to 'Torquils'. In later years the premises have housed a dress shop, a delicatessen (Le Cochon) and now a pizzeria.

George Day kept meticulous handwritten records and his Local Circular Register lists the names of the houses and their owners. Strict instructions were set out: *'The Register to be used in all cases of doubt for reference to spelling of names: All letters to be addressed to the lady occupier when this is possible and initials to be used where given: Where the name of the occupier is given as a gentleman only it should be addressed to him and not taken for granted that a lady is resident: In the case of a house with no name, and occupied, address as new house viz 'New House, Avon Road'.*

He certainly seemed to have been the leading supplier in the area for his delivery round was very extensive, covering all the roads in the immediate vicinity. His records contain three pages for Canford Cliffs Road and include Widdicombe Avenue, Haig Avenue and Lawrence Drive; the round took in Brudenell Road, Shore Road, Chaddesley Glen, virtually the whole of Sandbanks and a considerable part of Branksome Park. Through George Day's Local Circular Register it has been possible to confirm the existence of most of the roads, hotels and houses, with many of the names of the owners.

As a teenager, Mrs Christine Clarke (daughter of George S Day), knew the area very well; she attended The Church of the Transfiguration, was in the choir and helped Doris Cooper and Annette Bailey with the Sunday School. During her college holidays Mrs Clarke worked at 'Greystoke' in Marlborough Road (now Nairn Road) when the Reverend Brian Hession ran it as an hotel. 'Heathfield' on Cliff Drive was the home of the Reverend Canon Alex J Barff, whose son Frederick became a well-known missionary in Ruanda with the Bible and Christian Missionary Society, and had links with the Reverend Roy Hession, brother of Brian. Doris Cooper, a faithful member of The Church of the Transfiguration, was housekeeper to the Barff family for many years, knew the Hession family and finished her working life as housekeeper to a wealthy Quaker, Mr Baker in Spencer Road.

The shops remembered by Mrs Clarke include Hudson Brothers, a good general store, next to Malmesbury and Parsons' Dairies on the south side of Grand Parade. Also along there was a well patronised restaurant 'The Rowan Tree' - one daily customer was a Mrs Gillet, married to a diamond merchant, she lived at 'Chetwynd' on Canford Cliffs Road. The St. Clair Café was another popular rendezvous for several decades from the 1940s; this was on the corner with Cliff Drive where is now Goadsby and Harding, estate agents. In addition to Mr Short, there was another chemist on the opposite side, and Mrs Clarke believes it was run by a Mr Haynes - this may be the shop recently taken over by the Portman Building Society, which has been owned by Mr Penny, F E Griffin, Claude H F Barnetson, Pars & Company and in 1918 Edward H Taylor.

Lord and Lady Docker would visit Canford Cliffs during the summer months - they arrived in a large creamy-yellow car, and Mrs Clarke recalls that Lady Docker was always elegantly dressed; customers of her father, he always found them to be a most pleasant couple.

In the mid-1980s the village of Canford Cliffs suffered a decline in trade and a number of shops became, and remained, empty. The International Stores, next to the Telephone Exchange (now Threshers wine merchants) closed its doors in July 1986 after almost 50 years of trading, thus leaving the residents without a general food store. The Bournemouth Echo reported in the November that a new landlord had increased the rents of some of the shops so much that it was impossible for the owners to continue in business.

Canford Cliffs Village 1988. The date 1933 on the building marks George Day's new shop premises built by Mr Hillman.
Author's Collection .

However, a glimmer of hope appeared in December 1986 when Cullens, a chain convenience store centred around a delicatessen, opened in the old International Stores building, and survived for a number of years. Gradually, the empty shops were taken over by fresh tenants.

Shops and traders remembered during the last 20 - 30 years may well include 'Leval' who sold luxury lingerie, 'Sea Sales' yachting outfitters, 'The Galleon' - stationers, booksellers, gifts and toys, the ironmongers, 'Maxwells' the fruiterers, Mr Lamb at the 'Canford Manshop', antique shops (Mr Levine and Mr J Lobley) and 'Pets & Gardens'. In 1975 there were three estate agents - Fox & Sons, Rumsey & Rumsey and Richard Godsell; the number had increased to six in 2001 with Executive Homes, Fox & Sons, Goadsby & Harding, Andrew Key & Drummond, Atkins, and Berkeleys - previous occupants of their corner premises have been the Post Office and Tearooms, '58 Baker Street' - ladies fashions, and 'Arcadian Interiors'.

Barrie the Fish initially ran the fresh fish counter at Dingles Food Hall in Bournemouth, and when that closed he started his own fishmongers in Westbourne, opening his second wet fish shop at 16 Haven Road, Canford Cliffs in 1984. This filled the gap left when Charles Harrison's shop at number 32 closed; unfortunately, Barrie the Fish did not stay long in the village.

Mr P F Tanner, famous for his pork pies and Cumberland sausages, traded at 34 Haven Road for many years, queues formed regularly outside his shop and among his customers were stars from the Summer Shows. After Mr Tanner retired, Peter Jeffery took over and continued there for some time. Harry Dixon & Son were the other butchers on the same side; Mr Cyril Strong was the manager, and when the shop closed he opened his own business in Penn Hill, taking over from Vernon & Tear.

Two dress shops have been in Canford Cliffs for some time - Mrs Shaw had her business in Bournemouth's Westover Road before opening 'Berys' at number 38 in the village during the mid-1970s; around the same time Mrs Brickwood set up her business 'Iris' on the south side of Haven Road, and this was later owned by Mrs Tidd.

The Telephone Exchange, on the south side, between Maxwell Road and Cliff Drive, opened as a sub-exchange on 3rd November 1920, but the first telephone directory to include Canford Cliffs was dated September of that year - nine names were listed:-

Canford Cliffs	1	Mr L G Cosh at the Post Office
Canford Cliffs	5	E Crump, Compson, Bella Vista, Sandbanks
Canford Cliffs	7	Miss G M Burton - Blake Hill House
Canford Cliffs	34	B Cairns Wilson - Sandacres Lodge, Parkstone-on-Sea

Canford Cliffs	38	The Right Honourable Sir Ernest Cassels at Sandacres, Parkstone-on-Sea (This may well have been the forerunner of the Sandbanks Hotel)
Canford Cliffs	55	Canford Cliffs Hotel
Canford Cliffs	56	A H G Close - The Corner House, Canford Cliffs
Canford Cliffs	78	Stanley H Burgess - 'Athboy' on Cliff Drive
Canford Cliffs	105	Clifford P B Charles MRCS LRCP at Minterne Grange, Lilliput.

By 31st March 1922 Canford Cliffs had 116 lines with 142 telephone sets connected; and 737 lines with 978 sets attached at the end of March 1936. Mrs Gwen Pritchard was a telephonist at the Exchange on 3rd September 1939 when the Prime Minister announced that we were at war with Germany; like most other people she wondered what the future held for this country. It was not until May 1940 that the telephonists received their instructions should an invasion occur; between two and five girls were likely to be on duty at any one time together with perhaps one engineer in the apparatus room. If they heard German soldiers tramping up the stairs, they were to press the button linking the exchange to Bournemouth and pass the message 'Canford Cliffs closing down', thus all connections would be cut off, but the girls were to pretend that they were operating normally. Their supervisor was quite excited about it all, but Gwen Pritchard remembers with gratitude that this particular event did not occur.

The Mayors of Bournemouth and of Poole - Councillor J H Turner and Alderman A B Haynes, called each other on 3rd December 1949 to inaugurate the £330,000 Boscombe and Canford Cliffs Automatic Telephone Exchanges.

Canford Cliffs Village 1988. Telephone Exchange beside tree.
Author's Collection

CHAPTER SIX
REDMOOR SCHOOL – THE FITZ CLUB
THE SEA WITCH HOTEL

Continuing along Haven Road on the south side, on the corner with Cliff Drive in 1918 was St Hilaire School run by Miss Rudd. This was the junior section of Redmoor Girls School which had an address of 111 Canford Cliffs Road and 3 De Mauley Road. The playing fields occupied the space between Elmstead and Ravine Roads and an annual tennis tournament was held; Dick Hartley's childhood home overlooked these playing fields, and he remembers that the family always placed grandmother at one of the upper windows so that she could view the tennis from a good vantage point.

The property at 3 De Mauley Road, now Canford Cliffs Nursing Home, may date back to 1895. Still the Redmoor School in 1939, by 1961 it had been turned into the Teesdale Hotel run by F G Terrell and R E Stallworthy, and in the 1977 Poole Guide Mr and Mrs L Pearce were recommending their establishment as *ideally situated in its own grounds facing south with a beautiful garden, and completely free of traffic noise.* The 16 rooms all had Hot and Cold wash-basins, fitted carpets, interior sprung divans, electric fires, razor sockets and central heating. A laundry room was available from Monday to Friday, but regrettably pets could not be accommodated.

The open space which was the Redmoor School playing fields was described in auction particulars of 1898 as 'A Matchless Site' for the erection of an institution, convalescent home, public school, hydropathic establishment or other kindred purpose. It seems that this 'matchless site' did not attract any buyers for on Thursday 17th August 1905, at the newly opened Canford Cliffs Hotel, it was for auction once again, but this time with the suggestion that it could be used for development of small residences.

Returning to Haven Road, St Hilaire occupied a large site and appeared to be one of the only three properties shown on the 1889 plan of the Canford Cliffs Estate, together with 'Carkeel' (Norfolk Lodge Hotel) and 'Morwenstow' (Sutton House). The land now contains Merrow Chase and Haven Heights - these apartments are on the actual site of the original building and it is believed that Merrow Chase was the garden.

The Fitz Club (or the New Fitz's Club), at 41 Haven Road (Haven Heights) is remembered by many local folk, as is the glamorous Becky Dean who was co-proprietor with her husband Lawrence, between 1952 and 1987. It has been suggested that the Club was set up by them in the early 1950's, but other sources (including George S Day's Local Circular Register of Customers) indicate that The Honourable Mrs Eustace Fitzgerald owned and operated the Fitz Club during WWII, and was still there in 1950; she may have originally lived in The Avenue, Branksome Park, and is believed to have been the instigator of a 1950's Poole Pageant, run by the 'World's Pageant Master' Owen Lally in Poole Park.

We know, from an advertisement in the Parkstone Yacht Club 1955 Handbook, that the proprietress Becky Dean (late of the Chez Moi Club in London) was promoting 'a Mayfair Club in Canford Cliffs' and it is probable that a decision was made to call it 'The New Fitz's Club' when she became the new owner in 1952. A former Windmill Girl, Becky Dean is remembered as a most glamorous host, appearing every night in full evening gown and fur wrap to welcome her regular visitors, among whom were showbiz personalities.

The Club was described as 'a place where time stood still, it was like a freeze-frame from a wartime movie, and boasted an upside down clock with the hands ticking backwards'. Jimmy Cooper was the manager there for a short time before becoming the licensee of the Canford Cliffs Hotel, and remembered among the various musical entertainments provided were the Ivor Raymond Singers, famous radio artistes of the time.

The New Fitz's Club closed in 1987 and Becky Dean died at the age of 80 two years later. In 1988 a Bournemouth Echo reporter wrote *'plans to develop the site of a legendary Canford Cliffs cocktail bar as sheltered housing have been thrown out by the planners'*. The old property, once housing a school and a well-known Club became derelict, and an eyesore in the village until it was eventually fenced off from the road. The present apartments, Haven Heights, were built in the mid 1990s.

Two houses, 'Brownleaves' and 'The Holt' were once to be found in Haven Road before Bessborough Road, and the site on which now stands the Sea-Witch Hotel was sold, as plot 41, on 22nd October 1886, for £310.00 The sale took place at a Ballot in the Bijou Hall, Albert Road, Bournemouth, and the buyer was an ironmonger from Bournemouth, Charles William Brooke; a stipulation stated that the value of the proposed property should not be less than £750.00.

Listed in the 1918 Kelly's Directory as 'Sunnifielde' occupied by a Mrs Wheatcroft, and in 1939 by Thomas B Earl, it was for sale with Rumsey and Rumsey estate agents in May 1946 and was still a private house in 1947. By 1961 it had become the Sunnifielde Guest House run by Mrs A Macpherson and was listed simply as 'hotel' in 1967; at some stage after this it is believed that the name was changed to the Sea-Witch by a Mr Dudley North.

The Fitz Club in its dilapidated state 1988.
Author's collection

An advertisement in the 1977 Poole Guide tells us that it is now under new management and *'personal supervision is guaranteed by the resident proprietors Mr and Mrs H I Hughes and Mr P Hughes'*. Since that time there have been a fair number of owners - the Tucker family sold to Kathleen and Ian Symonds in 1985, next were Mr and Mrs Pike, and in 1990 John and Diane Rees were there for a few years. In a 1987/1988 brochure, the Two-Star establishment Sea-Witch Hotel (with Renoirs Restaurant) was offering 'en-suite accommodation with central heating, telephone, colour television, radio, tea/coffee making facilities and clothes press. New Free in-house movies (films) in rooms evening and week-ends'. The price per person per night for bed and breakfast ranged from £29.95 to £34.95. Before setting up their successful restaurant 'Harriets' in Lilliput, the Higgins family ran the Sea-Witch Hotel for a short while in the mid-1990s.

Of equal longevity is the Norfolk Lodge Hotel. One of the first sites on the Canford Cliffs Estate to be purchased, the house 'Carkeel' was built in 1886 on the corner plot between Haven and Bessborough Road; it was described as 'a gentleman's residence with servants quarters'. Only one other property had been built along that stretch of Haven Road from Flaghead Chine back towards Canford Cliffs Road at that time - this was 'Morwinstow', now called Sutton House.

On an Estate Plan of 1889 the corner plot opposite Norfolk Lodge on Bessborough Road was marked 'proposed site for church'. This is now 'Green Shutters', and the proposed site for the vicarage was next door to 'Carkeel' on Haven Road.

*Norfolk Lodge 1920s. Message on back of postcard '
We catch a 'bus at this lamp post which takes us to a tram at County Gates - which lands us in the town'. Courtesy: Mr Lewis Shaw*

It is possible that 'Carkeel' was turned into an hotel in 1930 and from the 1939 Kelly's Directory we learn that it was called Norfolk Lodge Boarding House run by Ames and Sons, who also supplied cars for hire. Well known in the area the establishment and taxi service was run as a family concern with Mr Ames and his wife Edna, their daughter Peggy and their son Ted and his wife.

Remembered by many local people, Philip C Pridmore and Charles W Fletcher bought the hotel in 1948 and only retired in 1983 when Alan and Jill Martin (who are still there) took over. A colourful advertisement in the 1977 Poole Guide states that the 'hotel stands in its own grounds of one acre right at the head of the lovely Flaghead Chine, with the beach 250 yards away'. The resident proprietors also offered home grown vegetables and fresh eggs from their own poultry, together with colour television.

When it was still possible to park your car in Bessborough Road whilst visiting the beach, the caged birds in the garden of Norfolk Lodge were always a colourful attraction. (Since this chapter was written a planning application has appeared for re-development into flats)

CHAPTER SEVEN
THE CLIFF DRIVE - ST CLAIR ROAD
HAVEN ROAD - IMBRECOURT

'The Cliff Drive' as it is marked on the 1889 site plan wanders around starting at the western end of the shops, passes the entrance to the Pleasure Grounds and The Chine, turns left at 'The Circle' to follow the cliff edge, does a tight right turn and ends at the junction with Flaghead Road and Bessborough Road, where it was once anticipated that a church would be built. There were no properties marked on the eastern side before The Esplanade in 1918, and only thirteen residents all told - these included on the north west side Lieutenant Lionel Owen Randolph Ashley at 'Flaghead', Martin H Sells at 'Pearlhaven' and Miss Canning at 'Chine Cottage'; on the south east side Mrs Hugh Taylor was at 'Canford Lodge', Hamilton W Thompson and Miss De Witte at 'Whiteley Wood' and on the north side Mrs Massey ran apartments at 'Canford House', Stanley H Burgess was at 'Athboy' (one of the nine names in the first Canford Cliffs telephone directory in 1920), Miss Darroch at 'Braidley', Mrs Hitchin at 'The Outlook', Charles Sharp Smith MRCS Eng. LSA Surgeon at 'Cliffe House', Mrs Clunes at 'The Rowans' and Cyril Owbridge at 'Cherry Garth'.

A collection of vehicles in front of 'Braidley' on Cliff Drive c 1940
Courtesy: Mr Ronald Pratt

By 1939 three houses had been built on the left before The Esplanade - 'Brampton Kinlet' (Jas Hargrave Simpson), 'The Sheiling' (Mrs M O'Neill East at number one and Alfred G Sainsbury at number two) and 'Balcormo' - mentioned elsewhere in this book is the fact that Dr Langran and his grandson were killed by a direct hit on this house in 1941, and it is believed that a lady and her daughter-in-law also died in one of the other properties. The younger lady was coming off duty, with a friend, from the Observation Post at the top of the Chine and decided to visit her mother-in-law, who during air-raids would sit alone under the stairs. As the daughter-in-law walked up the garden path, the bomb fell and they were both killed. Several UXB'S (unexploded bombs) also fell close by on that occasion, and one resident, who was living in Wootton Cottage on Cliff Drive (where is now 'La Corniche') found that her way home was cordoned off and she had to go the long way round to get there.

A Mr Alfred Hussy was a milk roundsman for Malmesbury and Parsons' Dairies and lived with his wife in a small property on Cliff Drive. Since it was a fair distance from Canford Cliffs to the depot on Sandbanks Road, Mr Hussy bought a car and, not having space for it at home, purchased a plot of land on the north side of Chaucer Road where he built himself a garage. One day during the war, having finished his round and put the car away, he walked home only to find that he didn't have a home - the house had gone and his wife killed by a direct hit. Bereft of both his home and his wife, Mr Hussy solved his accommodation problem by building a house around his garage, and this became the living room. Wishing to alleviate his loneliness he wrote to his wife's best friend at the Yorkshire shoe shop where they had both worked many years before; to his surprise a reply came by return - the friend had not married and had become manageress of the shop. In due time Mr Hussy married his wife's best friend and they continued to live in the house built around the garage, it was called 'Alfredie'. Eventually, the property was sold to Mr Charles Harrison, the fishmonger, who wanted to live close to his shop in the village.

'Orton Rigg' on Cliff Drive. Courtesy: Miss H Beckwith/Mrs H Baggaley

Opposite the Pleasure Grounds, by Bodley Road, a substantial property was built around 1895 for Sir John Archer KBE JP and Lady Archer. Still known by its original name of 'Orton Rigg', it is now an hotel run by the Arthritis Care organisation. One or two local folk remember that, in their childhood days, parties were held from Orton Rigg in the garden on the other side of Bodley Road when the butler used to cross backwards and forwards carrying jellies and other goodies to the waiting youngsters. One lad also recalls meeting Lady Archer, all ready dressed for her morning swim, as she went down The Chine.

The house was for sale through Rumsey & Rumsey, estate agents, on the instructions of Sir John Archer in August 1942, and by 1961 it had become the 'London Association for the Blind' Holiday Home with Miss M E Shelton as Matron, and by 1975 was described as the 'British Rheumatism and Arthritis Association' Holiday Home. Mrs Hazel Baggaley has been manager at the Orton Rigg Hotel for a number of years; several extensions have taken place including a spacious sun lounge opened in 1986 by the late Sir Joseph Weld.

One of the four establishments around the country under the heading of Arthritis Care, the Orton Rigg Hotel offers holidays for people with arthritis together with their families. Extra facilities are available for those who need them and, as in many other hotels, in-house entertainment is provided as well as outings to places of interest in their own luxury coach. Their brochure invites potential guests to enjoy the benefits of a holiday in an impressive Victorian mansion set in its own delightful south facing gardens.

Cricket enthusiasts may well recall the famous cricketer Wilfred Rhodes 1877-1973 who, in retirement, lived with his daughter and son-in-law (Mr and Mrs Burnley) at 4 Beaumont Road before his death in a Broadstone nursing home. He had an amazingly long career in cricket playing for Yorkshire from 1898 to 1930, until he was 53; he took more wickets for that County than any other bowler and scored 58 centuries. Playing for England from 1899 to 1926, Wilfred Rhodes averaged over 30 as a batsman and took 127 wickets in 58 Test Matches. His best performances were seven wickets for 17 runs against Australia in 1902, eight for 68 also against Australia the following Season. After his playing days were over he coached at Harrow School until gradually losing his sight. It is understood that John Arlott interviewed him on his 90th birthday.

The number of properties on Cliff Drive had risen to twenty eight by 1939 and included Miss Bradnack's school at 'Leas Court' and a guest house 'Canford' run by Campbell & Bird Limited. In recent years many of the original properties have been replaced by apartments, number eleven 'Ardmore' was of a distinctive Swiss chalet design, occupied by Doris Odlum MA MRCS LRCP DTM Physician and Surgeon, who is well remembered by many local folk.

A navigation light once adorned number nineteen Cliff Drive, which was the home of the late John Lobley; a few years ago he had the old property demolished with apartments then built on the site and he opted to occupy the penthouse - the navigation light still exists, but no longer serves its original purpose. Another historical artefact purchased by him was a very large pair of binoculars - like telescopes - mounted on an iron stand, which stood on the cliffs at Boulogne. Of German manufacture, the binoculars were brought to England as 'bounty' after the Germans had surrendered, and a story was told that Goering used them on the cliffs at Boulogne to view Folkstone. This tale was not believed until Mr and Mrs Lobley watched a film about D-Day ('The Longest Day') which contained German archive black and white film showing Goering arriving at Boulogne and looking through the binoculars.

As Squadron Leader of 210 Squadron Royal Air Force during WWII, John Lobley piloted flying boats from Poole and was later seconded from the RAF to Imperial Airways (later BOAC) to take VIP's on important flights. He took the relieving Governor and his staff to Singapore after the Japanese surrender and brought back the previous Governor who had been released from captivity. No navigational charts for Singapore were available at that time and John Lobley sent his co-pilot out to buy a school atlas - on their arrival the Sunderland flying boat circled several times trying to locate a suitable stretch of water on which to put down. At the last moment a launch appeared carrying a large banner with the message 'Follow Me'. For the return journey the seats of the Sunderland were stripped out so that stretchers could bring home some of the those who had been Japanese prisoners of war, many of whom were in a pitiful state after their years of misery.

Four motor cars at 'Braidley' on Cliff Drive
Courtesy: Mr Ronald Pratt

St. Clair Road contained ten properties in 1918 - five on each side, 'Stebonheath', 'Kinloch', 'Sonari', 'Bytheway', 'Rossclare', and 'Mowbray', 'Kilmuir', 'Canonbury', 'Chingford' and 'Miramar'. A dental surgeon, Mr Reginald Umney lived at 'Mowbray' and is remembered by one or two local residents; he was a Sheriff of Poole and died during his year of office in 1939. Five more houses had been built by 1939 - 'Stebonheath' had changed its name to 'Mindrim', 'Kinloch' was a private hotel (later Ebdon House) run by Mrs E Zipfel, and Mr R Umney was still at 'Mowbray'. The number of properties had risen to 29 in 1975.

'Stebonheath', now 'Mindrim', was one of the earliest properties on the Canford Cliffs Estate, known as plot 210 it was sold for £120.00 in 1889 but the building was not completed until November 1897; the purchaser was Mr Thomas Watkinson Archbutt of 11 Angell Road, Brixton, London. The design of the house, giving 'a good view of shipping in Poole Bay' was so impressive that a photograph of the house, together with its surrounding fence, was used to illustrate sale brochures for further plots on the Estate between 1900 and 1905. The heavy cast iron fence with an attractive design of vine leaves and grapes is very unusual and distinctive.

There is a suggestion, which has not been confirmed, that it may have come from a bridge in London spanning the River Thames - Vauxhall Bridge was demolished and re-built about the same time as the house was erected.

1930s view from St Clair Road - tennis court on left
Courtesy: Mr Ronald Pratt

'Morwinstow' in Haven Road was another of the very early properties and served as the Estate Office in 1886; a Mrs S R P Carver was there in 1918, the name is not listed in 1939 but may have been The Links Guest House. By 1961 it had become Sutton House Convalescent Home, and later was used as a holiday home for the staff of the Metal Box Company - it was converted into flats several years ago.

'Courtlands' in Haven Road dates back to the early 1900s, the Misses Thistlewood were in occupation in 1918 and The Reverend Claude Beckwith came, with his wife and family, to the property in 1931. He had retired early due to the ill-health of his wife, but gave generously of his time helping local clergy, serving on numerous committees and was the Scout Commissioner for Bournemouth. Miss Helen Beckwith remembers that in the early days their large garden was home to many farmyard animals, including a goat, which together with the dogs, would accompany the children on their walks down to the beach. Helen Beckwith herself gave a lot of time to helping Guide Companies and Brownie Packs in the area, including the Victoria School for Handicapped Children in Lindsay Road, and remembers the Guide Commissioner for Bournemouth, Miss Ethel Haberson, living on Cliff Drive in 1939.

In the 1930s the woods on the opposite side of Haven Road ran down to the golf course; the house 'Imbrecourt' which was further up towards what is now the roundabout, was occupied in 1918 by Mr Reginald Young, followed by Mr Charles Eysoldt and his mother. Knowledge of the house and of the area in the 1930s has been revealed through the diaries of Miss Margaret Tucker (later Mrs Margaret Fellows) who was Mrs Eysoldt's cook for several years.

Margaret Tucker was born at Fellside Cottage in Bingham Avenue, Lilliput, and began her working life at 'Grey Rigg' in Lilliput as a housemaid, where Lady Olave Baden-Powell lived as a young woman. Margaret worked with families in Chester and London before returning to Dorset in 1935, and after settling her parents into their retirement bungalow - her father had been head gardener at Grey Rigg for twenty five years - she scanned the Situations Vacant in the Bournemouth Echo. Two days after replying to Mrs Eysoldt's advertisement for a cook *'a chauffeur in livery arrives and asks me to go for an interview at Imbrecourt'*. Mrs Eysoldt tells Margaret what sort of cooking will be required and that there would be bridge parties and some entertaining; her son Charles had just bought Imbrecourt and she herself owned another house at New Milton, from whence most of the vegetables and summer fruit would arrive weekly. The staff at Imbrecourt consisted of a parlourmaid, single-handed housemaid, a chauffeur and a gardener; Margaret would be cooking for them as well as for Mrs Eysoldt and her son.

Before the end of the interview Margaret was given a guided tour of the house - the drawing room was beautifully furnished by Harvey Nicholls, the large lounge had lovely French windows opening on to the garden and lawn, the dining room led through to the staff sitting room and the well equipped modern kitchen. *'Mrs Eysoldt then took me up the front staircase and showed me the remainder of her beautiful home'*. As well as the room she would share with the housemaid, Margaret was shown the staff bathroom and other quarters, all of which were comfortably furnished. Her wage was to be £60.00 per year, and time off was every other Sunday afternoon and evening plus half a day in the week, to be back at home by 10.00pm. *'So, the interview over, Mr West the chauffeur drives me back to my home, and early the following week he arrives with a note to say my references are satisfactory and that on my first day Mr West would call for me and my luggage'.*

Margaret was introduced to Frances, the parlour maid and Bridget the housemaid, and her first few days were spent learning the routine of the household. Mrs Eysoldt would discuss the day's menus at 9.00am and indicate what should be ordered from which tradesmen - the bread was delivered by a Mr Lloyd from Bournemouth Road, the milk and cream from 'the well-known' farm of Purchase and Vine at Wallisdown, Mrs Eysoldt usually bought the poultry and meat joints herself when out shopping in the Daimler and the fish came from the village fish shop of Mr Charles Harrison. The staff meals were similar to the dining room with traditional roasts, steak and kidney pies and puddings, meat casseroles or poultry, followed by a variety of sweets.

Apparently Mrs Eysoldt was fond of fruit pies, rice dishes and fritters, and when Mr Charles was home at the week-end from London his favourite dishes were prepared and served. He liked smoked salmon, dover sole stuffed with shrimps, fresh Christchurch salmon when in season, and steaks and fillets of veal; his favourite sweets included cold chocolate souffles, fruit flans, meringues, apfelstrudel and brandy snaps filled with cream. Preparation for Mrs Eysoldt's bridge parties included the baking of scones, making of plain and fancy cakes, and home made fillings for the sandwiches - chicken, salmon or sardines would be passed through a fine sieve and mixed with butter or cream. Frances, the parlour maid, would help Margaret cut the bread, and butter the bridge rolls ready to receive their fillings. Afterwards they would always be thanked by Mrs Eysoldt for their successful handling of the event.

On the occasions when the lady of the house spent a day in London, being taken to Bournemouth Central Station by the chauffeur early in the morning, Margaret was allowed to provide lunch for her parents at Imbrecourt and they were chauffeured both ways by Mr West.

Christmas and the New Year meant a great deal of extra work for Margaret but her diary records that it was an enjoyable time. *'The festive season was a great do, the Yule tree was 10 to 12 feet high and reached up to the upstairs front landing, gaily decorated, it held presents for one and all. Mrs Eysoldt's friends stayed at the house until the New Year; other friends from London went to The Hawthorns Hotel in Bournemouth* (now the Wessex Hotel on the West Cliff) *and came to Imbrecourt for lunch and dinner. Mr Charles enjoyed entertaining them with his cine-camera and during the day, weather permitting, they all loved to walk along the beach'.*

Easter was also a busy time with more visitors - the traditional English Saddle of Lamb on Easter Sunday, and the cooking of batches of Hot Cross Buns, served hot for breakfast on Good Friday and later toasted and buttered for afternoon tea. Mrs Eysoldt would depart to London for a few days afterwards, enabling the staff to spring clean the house.

In her off duty time Margaret would cycle to see her parents, and learnt to skate at the Westover Ice Rink to the music of Percy Pearce, a well known orchestra of the time; at a later stage she enjoyed old time dancing at the Bournemouth Pavilion. All the staff were allowed to take their two weeks holiday during the summer and Margaret travelled to Devon on a Royal Blue Coach from Bournemouth to stay with relatives, who were farmers on the edge of Dartmoor. *'My summer holiday is now over and I return once again to Imbrecourt, feeling well and sun-tanned after a lovely time. As autumn days come along Mrs Eysoldt is busy arranging her bridge parties and I prepare the ingredients ready to make the Christmas cake and puddings so that it allows time for them to mature before the festive season'.*

During the autumn of 1936 Margaret becomes a member of the Canford Cliffs Women's Institute which meets at the village hall each month; any spare time in the evenings is spent knitting matinee coats to be given to the maternity wards at the Cornelia Hospital (forerunner of Poole Hospital in Longfleet Road). The doctor's wife, Mrs Langran from Cliff Drive, bought the wool (white and blue) and collected the finished items at the same time as leaving more wool for further knitting. Margaret and the maids did not have the spare time for this at the week-ends as *'Mr Charles would arrive from London in time for dinner on Friday evenings, and always his favourite dishes were served, and on Saturdays and Sundays there were usually friends for meals. The Sunday evening meal was quite simple - soup, cold poultry or meat and salad with a cold sweet, cheese, biscuits and coffee'.*

In 1938 Mrs Eysoldt's health deteriorated; she had an operation in London and returned home accompanied by two nurses. All the staff were sad when she died, and their sympathy was with Mr Charles in the loss of his mother.

Life at Imbrecourt is much quieter and the parlour maid decides to seek another position, leaving Bridget and Margaret to keep the household running smoothly; Mr Charles sometimes stays in London during the week and they often exercise his 'faithful mongrel dog'. *'We usually take the walk through Flaghead Chine and along the beach to Shore Road and return via Chaddesley Woods and the main road to the house. During these walks we pass the construction work being carried out between Simpson's Folly and Shore Road and the foreman always smiled and passed the time of day and the men always gave us a smile too. I had no idea that one of them later on was to become my husband'.*

Royal Blue Charabanc - believed to be a Parkstone Gardeners' Outing 1920s. Young fellow in bobble hat is Ronald Pratt, standing immediately behind him in trilby hat is Mr Middleton, Head Gardener at Compton Acres.
Courtesy: Mr Ronald Pratt

Her sister was a member of the Belstone (Devon) Women's Institute and in 1939, before the outbreak of WWII, had been elected as their delegate for the Rally to be held at The Royal Albert Hall in London, and Margaret was able to accompany her. *'It was a great event and was addressed by Mr Walter Eliot, who I think was Health Minister at that time, and I shall never forget the singing of their song Jerusalem, it rang through the massive building'.*

Margaret writes of the grim happenings abroad as the summer progresses, and of Neville Chamberlain's trips to Munich. *'Early September we hear the sad news on the radio we are at war, it was indeed a sorrowful announcement and I remember how intently we listened to every news bulletin. Everyone was eager to do what they can to help, our three Services were at the alert, the Red Cross and all the medical services were at the ready, and the Fire Service and all departments of the Civil Service. Factories were running at full speed, and tasks which were not of national importance were stopped; so Bridget and I no longer see the "boys" on the construction work at Shore Road, as the job was called to a halt and they went off to help the war effort.*

Margaret's usual autumn routine of making the Christmas cakes and puddings was achieved, but in December early one morning she had an unfortunate accident, tripping on the stairs, falling to the bottom and hitting a cupboard. A broken collar bone was suspected and the milkman, who was a member of the St. John Ambulance Brigade placed the arm in the correct position and put it in a sling. As soon as Mr Charles was told of the accident, he telephoned Dr Risk (living either in The Esplanade or Lavender Cottage), who came along and advised

Margaret to go to the Outpatients Department of the Cornelia Hospital for the injury to be strapped up, and she was taken there by Mr West in the Daimler. As it was her left arm which was affected Margaret was able to carry on with most of her duties, and she received plenty of help from the rest of the staff. The icing of the Christmas cake posed a problem but help was forthcoming from her mother and Mr Lloyd the baker.

Christmas 1939 was quiet as it was, not only the first one since Mrs Eysoldt's death, but also the first *festive season* of the war. In the New Year Mr Charles decided they needed a large air-raid shelter: Mr Hillman, the Canford Cliffs builder carried out the work, excavating a bank outside the kitchen window which faced across Parkstone Golf Course. Containing four rooms, it appears that the shelter took a year to build. Despite the war, Margaret and a friend were able to take a cycling holiday in the summer of 1940 visiting friends and relatives in Somerset and Devon.

As enemy action in the Poole area became more frequent, Margaret worried about her parents, who lived near the Alderney area of Parkstone, and she cycled up to see them whenever possible. *'One day I met one of the men who had been on the construction work at Shore Road - he was on his way to Branksome Station to catch the train to Holton Heath where he was then doing war work on a shift basis. He seemed pleased to see me again and we arranged to meet, and so our romance began and we married eighteen months later'*. On 1st March 1941 Margaret informed Mr Charles of her forthcoming marriage and gave one month's notice.

Over thirty years later (1973 or 1974) Margaret reads of the death of Mr Charles Eysoldt and recollects the happy years she spent working at Imbrecourt. *'Now it is sad to see the lovely house is no more as the grounds are prepared for the construction of new properties. As the years go by one learns to accept progress and new development and to realise that when the new buildings are completed, that many occupants will be able to enjoy the lovely views over Poole Harbour, Lilliput, and the golf course. As time passes, changes take place in the Canford Cliffs area, some of the larger houses are demolished to make way for luxurious flats and modern bungalows, but all seem to blend well with the existing properties, and it remains as beautiful as ever and is often referred to in the newspapers as the 'Diamond Ring' area'*.

CHAPTER EIGHT
CANFORD CLIFFS ROAD – COMPTON ACRES
FORSYTE SHADES

From Imbrecourt, Canford Cliffs Road runs northwards to Penn Hill Corner. A long road, it was once little more than a track known as Sandy Lane, and some sources mention the first part of it as Award Road. In 1918, under West Bournemouth, only four properties were listed - 'Minnigaff', 'Redmoor School', 'The Glen', and 'Woodneuk'; by 1939 over 70 properties were numerated along the whole road from Haven Road to Archway Road. This number had grown to 120 in 1961 and Redmoor School for Girls had been converted into flats; apartment blocks 'Moonrakers' and 'Carisbrooke' had appeared in 1975 and Redmoor had gone.

An unhappy event occurred at a house in Canford Cliffs Road in 1941 during a WWII air raid. Frank James of James & Sons Estate Agents lived there with his family, and on the night in question had made arrangements to visit his mother in Bournemouth, having forgotten that his brother and family were coming to see them that evening. He, therefore, telephoned his mother to postpone his visit; when the air raid siren wailed that evening the two families all headed for the shelter at the end of the garden. After a while they began to feel cold, and the two brothers crossed the lawn to collect blankets and warm clothing from the house. The property received a direct hit and the two men were killed.

Returning to the southern end of the road at the junction with Lilliput Road is to be found the internationally famous Compton Acres Gardens. A freehand map *'A Plan of Lands at Parkson belonging to Sir Thomas Webb and Mr Thomas Cload, Heath West of the Manor of Great Canford'* dated 20th July 1748 shows a spot marked 'Compton Acre', roughly situated between the modern Lilliput and Canford Cliffs.

A Conveyance dated 20th February 1914 refers to The Right Honourable Bertie Baron Wimborne, The Right Honourable Richard George Penn Earl Howe, The Right Honourable William Henry Baron de Ramsey and John Buchanan Marshall McMeekin; a further Conveyance dated 9th August 1917 records the name of Thomas Walter Simpson with that of Mr McMeekin.

Mr T W Simpson was the creator of the Gardens between 1918 and 1920, and conceived the idea of surrounding the house with a unique series of separate independent gardens, so planned that only one could be seen at a time. Subsequent owners were Mr J Stanley Beard JP,

Mr John Brady, Mr Lionel Green, and since 1999 three local families - the Harrisons, the Pikes and the Taylors under the heading of Red Sky Leisure Limited.

Mr Ben Boothby, a privileged friend of Mr Simpson and a constant visitor to the Gardens, compiled a set of hand-written volumes describing Compton Acres and their history and wrote in his foreword: *'What strikes the visitor to the gardens of Compton Acres most is their entirely restful dignity and peace, even as much as their colourful glory. It is difficult to realise that they are but a comparatively recent evolution from wild moorland to sylvan walks, smooth lawns, noble terraces, lily ponds, fountains and tumbling rills usually found only in gardens of great age. In this year of grace 1939 I am impelled to carry my memory back over a least half a century; when, with my brothers, I was wont to chase the elusive lizard and butterfly over this very same spot. What is now Canford Cliffs Road was then little more than a track known as 'Sandy Lane' winding over moorland unsurpassed for charm. It was a wilderness of golden gorse, purple heather and wind-swept bushes, hills of yellow sand rich with coarse russet-brown grass; steep gorges of orange and red sand with banks densely clad in Scots Pines over whose tops gleamed the blue waters of Poole Harbour, and in the far distance the ever-changing Purbeck Hills. Not a house to be seen save Brownsea Castle nestling among its green trees; and scacely a living creature; the summer air laden with those exquisite warm scents that go with bracken, heather and pines'.*

The original house at Compton Acres
Courtesy: John Etches of Bournemouth

It took several years of inspired planning, intense activity, and the expenditure of about £220,000 before the Gardens evolved. Thousands of tons of stone, rocks and good soil were brought from far and wide. Rare plants, many tropical and sub-tropical, together with wrought iron gates, bronze and marble statuary, lead figures and vases, fountains, well heads, lanterns and carved stone benches, many of them museum pieces, were collected from all parts of the world.

In the early years the Gardens were only open to the public on Saturdays. Mr William George, who lived in Spencer Road and was involved with many local activities, was a friend of Mr Simpson and Mrs Eileen Greenhill, daughter of Mr George, remembers that her father manned one of the two entrance gates, her mother was in charge of the tea room and she herself acted as a waitress. There is a suggestion that her father gave Mr Simpson some of the fish from their own pond, and one supposes that those now swimming around at Compton Acres might just be descendants of those original fish.

WWII took its toll - gardeners went into the Armed Forces or essential war work and towards the end of the hostilities Middleton, the famous Head Gardener, died. Once the war was over in 1945 and work could have re-started, the creator of Compton Acres, Mr T W Simpson himself died; the Gardens deteriorated and became overgrown, and several years of neglect followed.

An auction of the property was held at St Peter's Hall in Bournemouth on Tuesday 16th September 1947, the joint auctioneers being Messrs Way and Waller and Messrs Jackson-Stops and Staff. *'A Well-Appointed, Dignified Residence in one of the finest positions in the district. Overlooking Poole Harbour and the Purbeck Hills there are four reception rooms, 13 bed and dressing rooms, five bathrooms and good Domestic Offices and extraordinarily fine and varied Gardens probably unsurpassed in the country'.* The total area was about 11.5 acres, or to be precise 11 acres, one rood and 30 poles. Four cottages were included in the sale - Mrs Middleton was in South Lodge, Mr Pickett in North Lodge, Mr R Gritten in South Cottage and Mr Curson in North Cottage.

Under the heading of General Remarks in the auction particulars mention is made of the 'omnibus service past the main gates thus bringing all the unexcelled amenities of Bournemouth within easy reach'. The Borough of Poole Rateable Assessment was £372.00 and the Rates 18/10d (.94p) in the Pound; the garden ornaments, seats and garden statuary were included in the Sale as well as the pump to drive the fountains and the benefit of a small War Damage Claim in respect of the glasshouses was to be passed to the purchaser. Descriptions of the Gardens include mention of the Terrace Lawn, the Palm Court, Desert and Water Garden and The Dell as well as 'the dainty prettiness of the Japanese Garden, the grandeur of the Italian Garden, the green peacefulness of the English Garden, and the primness of the Dutch Garden'.

The house and gardens did not sell at auction and it was not until 1950 that Mr J Stanley Beard JP, a London architect, bought Compton Acres in order to spend his retirement years restoring and reconstructing the Gardens. For 18 months it was a hive of industry - tree-felling, thinning out and pruning was followed by many structural alterations and replanting. The house was restored and the gardeners' cottages repaired and modernised.

Compton Acres was then re-opened to the public in May 1952 by the Mayor of Poole, Miss Mary Llewellin JP (of Upton House). From a 1962 Guide Book, which cost 1s.0d (.05p), we learn that the admission charge was 3s 0d (.15p) with children under 14 half price, and descriptions were given of The Glen, Rock and Water Gardens, The Lawns and Terrace, The Heather Dell, Japanese, Roman, English and Italian Gardens and The Palm Court. What was once a 'picnic arbour' was re-designed in 1956/7 and dedicated as a memorial to the three children of John Beard and his wife May. Two daughters Anne and Elizabeth died of polio aged 28, and Dick was killed, at the age of 20, while flying with the Royal Air Force in WWII. The Garden of Memory is still a secluded sanctuary providing an area for rest and reflection.

Changing hands in 1964, Compton Acres was bought by a wealthy businessman, Mr John Brady, who it is believed made his fortune in the upholstery business in the Midlands. He and his family lived in the house for more than 20 years and as well as maintaining and improving the Gardens he added a shop and restaurant. Mr Brady donated generously to charities, and after selling the house and Gardens retired to Spain.

March 1986 saw the opening episode of 'The Collectors' on BBC 1 Television. 'A fast-moving 10-part series venturing behind the closed doors of a Custom and Excise Operation', filming took place in and around Poole which was named 'Wrelling' for the series. Locations in this area included Salterns Marina, Harbour Heights Hotel, Holy Angels Church and Compton Acres - the house was the residence of one of the main characters and many scenes were shot in the Gardens. The public were not barred whilst filming was in progress and one particular shot on The Terrace overlooking the Harbour had over 200 visitors, off camera, watching the scene and some had to be restrained from walking in front of the camera. During the filming of 'The Collectors', the news broke that Compton Acres was once again on the market.

View from Compton Acres in 1962

It was purchased in 1986 by a London property developer, Lionel Green, who expanded the Gardens and created wheelchair access to all parts. Permission was granted for the house to be demolished and 78 flats built, together with five luxury homes, and an Agreement was reached with the new owner that Compton Acres would be handed over to the Borough of Poole should the Gardens not be properly maintained, thus ensuring their continuity for future generations.

The contents of the house were auctioned in 1987, and a lady who had been browsing through a rail of gentlemens' clothes, found £500 in £20 notes in one of the pockets - this was handed back to Mr Brady's family. The house was demolished soon after the auction.

The building of the flats, known as Chartcombe, took place in 1988 and a brochure produced by the developers described them as 78 elegant one and two-bedroom apartments designed for retirement living, and offering the best of modern security and convenience. *'The inner core of this unique development is a dramatic atrium rising through three galleries creating a soaring shaft of light dappled by hanging plants and epitomising the perfection of Chartcombe. The spectacular vistas over the surrounding gardens, the magnificent sweep of Poole Harbour, and the pure tranquillity of Compton Acres Gardens themselves have created the ultimate retreat for retirement living'*.

Residents at Chartcombe were to have the benefit of a private gate into the Gardens, which could be used during the hours they were open to the public. A restriction was that one occupier of each apartment must be aged 60 years or over.

The first Head Gardener was Mr Middleton who died towards the end of WWII (1939-1945) but it is not known who took his place when Mr J Stanley Beard was in residence. Geoff Smith was Head Gardener for 24 years from 1964, and now John Heron has that position; his diverse background covers horticulture and landscape design at Merrist Wood College and with Hillier Nurseries. Arriving at Compton Acres in 1991, first of all as Assistant Head Gardener, John Heron holds workshops on all aspects of gardening and has been part of the team which offers school children the opportunity of enjoying some of the educational aspects of the Gardens.

When Lionel Green decided to sell Compton Acres in 1999 three local families, who had all enjoyed visiting the Gardens in their childhood, joined together and purchased Compton Acres - brothers Nigel and Keith Harrison, Adrian and Alexander Pike and Peter and Jayne Taylor. Recently the Canadian Woodland Walk was created together with 'Off The Beaten Track Nature Trail' to encourage youngsters to enjoy and appreciate our natural world.

New in 2001 has been the opening of the Deer Sanctuary in which a group of muntjacs, Britain's smallest species of deer, live in a spacious and secure woodland area; construction of a Tree Top Lookout enables visitors to observe the deer without disturbing them. A new restaurant, overlooking the Italian Garden, will soon be open and will have a separate entrance.

Compton Acres has always been a source of considerable interest to the media - way back in the summer of 1955 a film of the Gardens in technicolour was made by a Mr Horace Shepherd with a commentary by Alvar Liddell, a well known BBC Newsreader; apparently the film was shown in cinemas throughout the then British Commonwealth. Our own local paper, the Daily Echo, always provides up-to-date information about events at Compton Acres, and in August 1975 reported temperatures in the 90s - *'Goldfish are being given the cold kiss of life to save them from death in the heatwave. At Compton Acres, half-hundredweight blocks of ice are being put into the 12 ornamental pools at night to bring down the temperature of the water. Several thousand fish are gasping as the water temperature soars'.*

Around the corner from Compton Acres, in Lilliput Road, is the entrance to the prestigious apartments 'Forsyte Shades'. Pevsner gave a brief description of the original house *'confident neo-Georgian of 1935 (built as Jubilee House)'*, and what is now the car park for Compton Acres was the driveway to the property passing North Lodge Cottage, which still stands.

The listing for Canford Cliffs Road in the 1939 Kelly's is under Bournemouth and at number 168 Mr S H Wall resided - at Forsyte Shades Cottage was Charles William Roberts, who came under the heading of Compton Acres at number 170. Mr John Clark purchased the house in 1945 for £15,000; as it was above the 15th green of Parkstone Golf Club Mr Clark had been under the impression that the Club might have wanted the property to use as their Clubhouse. This was not so and he sold it in 1948 before buying Poole Harbour Yacht Club (Salterns Hotel and Marina). See 'Looking Back at Lilliput' by the author.

In 1961 Lady Watson was listed as occupying Forsyte Shades, and in the Cottage was The Honourable Mrs J M E Southwell. The house was demolished in 1974 and the apartments —18 flats and three penthouses - were built soon after. The original property had an extensive garden and many of the old paths and walks are still enjoyed by the residents.

CHAPTER NINE
NAIRN ROAD – ST. ANN'S HOSPITAL REVEREND BRIAN HESSION

Returning to Imbrecourt, the cul-de-sac named after the old house contains a number of properties and is to be found at the junction of Canford Crescent and Nairn Road. Only two houses were listed for Canford Crescent in 1918 - Mrs Waterhouse at Red Gables and Mrs Cowper Reed at Firlands; this had risen to seven properties by 1939 with the addition of Marlborough Cottage and Ellerslie on the east side and Compton Cottage, The Berea and Darville on the west. In 1975 there were sixteen properties.

Part of Nairn Road was once called Marlborough Road and in 1918 four properties existed - Maryland, Greystoke, Greystones and Tredinnoc with eight in 1939 now including Corvesgate and Corvesgate Cottage, Villa Sant Antonio, Watergate, Wolryche, The Grove and The Knoll; Sir Leonard Lyle JP was at Greystoke. That which was Nairn Road in 1939 had on the south side, Miss H M Ogden at Gorsehill with Percy H Muller at Sarum House and Herbert Adams at Nairn Cottage on the north side. By 1961 the name Marlborough had disappeared and Nairn Road ran from Canford Crescent to Haven Road, with 21 residences and several apartment blocks, and the previous home of Sir Leonard Lyle had become the Greystoke Hotel, standing between Island View and Coral Gables, occupied by the Reverend Brian Hession; by 1975 this site was occupied by Cliftons.

The house Greystoke was built in 1911 with walls of purple brick and a dark coloured roof. Sale particulars (circa 1920) from a London Agent, Mr J D Garrett, give interesting information about the property, and it is possible that Lord Lyle was the purchaser at this time. He was Chairman of the West Indies Sugar Company, President of Tate & Lyle and Member of Parliament for Bournemouth during the years of WWII (1939-1945).

Greystoke stood in four acres on a *'beautiful hill-site with magnificent views from the South and South West Fronts of Poole Harbour, Corfe Castle and Branksea Island'*. The large hall had oak pillars and staircase and an anthracite stove, the downstairs rooms - dining, drawing and morning - had oak parquet floors and mahogany doors with glass handles. As well as central heating *'the chimneys all draw well and never smoke'*. There were eleven bedrooms, three bathrooms and three boxrooms.

Of particular interest was the 'Organ in the Hall', described as *'Roll Playing; With Manual; In Two Parts; by Messrs Vincent Willis'*. The Great and Upper Organ was a Console, standing alone in the Hall between the two, so that the player could hear conveniently. The 3hp Electric Motor was outside the house to eliminate the sound of dynamo; the Bellows and part of the Organ were in the cellar below the Hall. *Twenty-one Speaking Stops; Two Swells; Four Combination Pneumatic Buttons and One Full Organ Pedal.* The Great Organ had 65 Pipes to each Stop and fourteen were listed ranging from Gemshorn through Melodia Bass to Tremulant; the Upper Organ had 48 Pipes to each Stop and 10 were listed from Musette to Lieblich Gedacht.

'Greystoke' in Nairn Road, once home of Sir Leonard Lyle and later an hotel owned by the Reverend Brian Hession. Courtesy: Mrs Margaret Traves

The architect was a Mr Tugwell, and during the days of Sir Leonard Lyle the house had squash and tennis courts, together with a swimming pool and a personal petrol pump. It seems that this was not unusual since filling stations were few and far between, and in fact it is believed that there was another privately owned pump in Martello Park at one time.

In due time Greystoke became an hotel and was owned by the Reverend Brian Hession, who later may have run it as a nursing home. He was known for his courageous fight against cancer; after his first major operation in 1954, he was told by the doctors that he had only a few days to live. It was in 'humble thanksgiving' for his recovery then that he founded Cancer Anonymous, an organisation to help victims to campaign for better diagnosis and treatment of the disease.

A graduate of Christ's College, Cambridge he was ordained priest in 1934 and after a spell as an R.A.F. Chaplain, was vicar of Holy Trinity Church, Walton 1937-1950. During most of this time he was active as a pioneer of religious films in Britain and in 1938 became founder and director of the Dawn Trust, a non-profit making organisation devoted to making religious films, which had its headquarters in Parkstone. He was also director of Bible Films 1945-1950. Of all

'This Is Your Life' - from left Eammon Andrews, Dr Payne, Brian Hession and Mrs Hession
Courtesy: Mrs Margaret Traves

the films with which he was connected, the one which attracted perhaps the widest attention was 'I Beheld His Glory', a full length colour film of The Crucifixion, which was shown for four weeks in London in 1953.

He is remembered mainly for his courageous refusal to submit to cancer; after each major operation, he plunged as quickly as possible back into his work of lecturing, writing and broadcasting. His book 'Determined To Live' published in 1956 had two reprints and a revised edition in 1958, as well as being published in America. A further book 'Bridge to God' told of his experiences and his faith.

Brian Hession and his family rented a cottage at Goathorn on Poole Harbour, and in 1948 he made and provided the commentary for a film *'Message (or Letter) from Goathorn'* which shows various aspects of Poole Harbour at that time - flying boats, the working port, old Poole characters and the sailing boats. Another of his films *'Ancient Stones'* was about Dorset Churches, including Wimborne Minster.

A local newspaper report on 22nd July 1948 describes Brian Hession's light hearted comments with reference to a Saturday outing to Poole by the choir of his Aylesbury Church - it appears that they decided to visit the area after watching his film. *'Had they gone to Brighton they would have only mooched round the shops or sat on the beach'*. To people coming from a land-locked town like Aylesbury, the sight of the Quay with all the boats alongside was stimulating. They were intrigued by the 'Hommes' and 'Dames' notices, which apparently are for the benefit

St. Ann's Hospital. Courtesy: Mr Lewis Shaw

of Norman and Breton seafarers. Their lunch at the King Charles Inn at 2s.0d. (10p) proved to be worth every penny, including coffee; a trip round the Harbour was 2s.0d (10p) with Mr Hession doing the commentary, and then back to the King Charles for tea at 1s.6d (7p). The choir had been looking forward to visiting the Town Museum for sixpence (3p) and Poole Pottery, but this was not to be. These comments from Mr Hession were quoted in the newspaper article *'Were either of these two things available to them? Not on your life. Why on Saturday, the one day when Poole receives most of its visitors, the Town Museum is solemnly shut, I don't know. This I consider a complete lack of imagination. Poole ought to go to it in the summer and particularly on a Saturday to push out the proverbial boat, put on its smartest coat and catch the imagination of visitors'.* He also commented upon the lack of benches along the quayside. Despite these pointed observations, Mr Hession thanked Poole for having them - *'they had a marvellous day and were determined to return for a longer stay'.*

The Reverend Brian Hession died in 1961 aged 52 years.

The address of St. Ann's Hospital is Haven Road in Canford Cliffs, but some years ago it was in West Road. This is not to say that it moved but the name of the road changed - that part of Haven Road from the top of Flaghead Chine down to Shore Road was originally known as West Road or West Hill. A Grade II listed building Pevsner describes it thus: *'A remarkable and severe building of 1910-1912 by the Scottish Arts architect Robert Weir Schultz. It is boldly composed on the clifftop, with splayed wings and long balconies on brick piers; dark red brick with shaped gables, Georgian windows, and much balustrading of pierced brick. The dormers have a slightly Scottish flavour, and on the entrance side there is a separate forebuilding with a cupola. There is a nice tile-hung lodge'.*

Initially connected with the Holloway Sanatorium in London, it has been suggested that a Cornishman who made a fortune from patent medicines in the mid-1800s sought to use his wealth for philanthropic purposes. Advice was sought from Lord Shaftesbury, who pointed out that mental health was always an important issue; the Cornishman proceeded to build, first of all, a hospital in Surrey followed later by the Holloway Sanatorium.

The Board of Management decided to prepare a seaside branch in the early 1900s and the Canford Cliffs site was selected; St. Ann's was closely associated with the parent hospital for the first thirty five years, and its patients came from the Holloway Sanatorium.

The heading under St. Ann's Sanatorium, West Road, Canford Cliffs in Kelly's Directory for 1918 informs us that William David Moore MD was Medical Superintendent, C.E. Campbell Williams MA MD visiting Medical Officer and Miss F E M Palmer, Matron; whilst in 1939, still under the heading of West Road, Harry Devine OBE MD FRCP was Medical Superintendent and Miss G M Lowe was Matron - Alfred J. Neville was at St. Ann's Lodge, William Morton at West Lodge, St. Ann's and George H. Grover was at Pine Cottage.

Policy changed in 1947 when it became an open hospital with far more informality. With the advent of the National Health Service, the Holloway Sanatorium and St. Ann's formed a group of the South West Metropolitan Region. St. Ann's was classified as an amenity and permitted to accept patients from any part of the country. Since the South West Metropolitan Region eventually became too large and unwieldy, a sub-division took place in 1959 with the establishment of the Wessex Region run from headquarters in Winchester. As a result of this change St. Ann's was, in 1960, disassociated from the Holloway Sanatorium and became part of the Herrison Hospital Group. Now part of the Dorset Healthcare NHS Trust, St. Ann's Hospital is a 133 bed acute admission facility for those requiring in-patient treatment, and covers the population of East Dorset.

The heading in the 1961 Kelly's Directory is now Haven Road. It is described as St. Ann's Hospital (Group No.52 Hospital Management Committee) with David Neil Parfitt MD MRCP DPM Consultant; W.Norman Crow BA MB ChB Physician-in-Charge; Miss A Neville - Matron. St. Ann's Lodge, West Lodge and Pine Cottage were occupied by some of these.

St. Ann's stands on what estate agents would call a prestigious site on the cliff top, and the grounds run down to the sea between Flaghead Chine and Shore Road. In recent years land bordering Haven Road has been sold to developers and there are a number of large houses within the old grounds, with an address of Chaddesley Pines.

CHAPTER TEN
HARBOUR HEIGHTS HOTEL
THE CONNING TOWERS

Panoramic, superlative, glorious, outstanding, breathtaking - these are some of the adjectives used over the years to describe the views from the Harbour Heights Hotel in Haven Road. On an 'island site' of five acres originally running down to Shore Road, the 1930s style property with white cement exterior has been a landmark, whether seen from Sandbanks or Shore Road, the sea or the air, for many years. It is no surprise to read that at one time the telegraphic address was 'Wonderview'.

East Looe House - Harbour Heights Hotel.
Line drawing by John Liddell from advertisement in an old Poole Guide.

Its history appears to date back around 100 years, for in 1901 the then landowner, Lord Wimborne, conveyed the site to a Mr R G Peck for £1875.00. The original residence built there was 'East Looe' and was sold in 1920. A magazine article dated 1935-6 gives information about 'The Harbour Heights Estate' near Bournemouth (Architects A J Seal & Partners of Bournemouth) - which covered the hotel, Harbour Court, the Conning Tower, Harbour Close (two rows of single-storey flat roofed terrace houses) and a house called 'Breydon'.

Pevsner described it as a *'brave and enterprising group of early modern buildings, admirably sited, with prominent glazed staircase curves derived from Mendelsohn'*; it is believed that the Conning Tower still retains such a staircase. A site plan indicates that the part of Chaddesley Glen from Haven Road (it was West Road at the time) to the first corner, was Church Road and originally ran straight down past the Church of the Transfiguration to Shore Road. This was deemed to have too steep a gradient for motor traffic and was kept as a footpath.

'East Looe' probably became a private hotel in 1920 and was enlarged in 1934 when it acquired the flat roof and white exterior. A recent book published in 2000 'Lives and Times of the Mayors of Bournemouth' tells us that Cliff Mattocks and his wife Joyce established the Harbour Heights Hotel overlooking Poole Harbour; his father Tom had been a Bournemouth Councillor and his grandfather William Mattocks had been Mayor 1897-8. The family had close connections with several Bournemouth hotels - The Tralee in St Michael's Road, Cliff Cottage in Beacon Road, Meyrick Cliffs Hotel and the Westminster Hall.

No information can be found for the intervening years, until 1939 when Kelly's Directory tells us that a Miss R C Seal was proprietress. Then came WWII when the hotel was requisitioned by the Air Ministry and at one stage was the Officers Mess for 210 Squadron. Previous occupants had been Australian Servicemen who had removed the three large capital 'H's from the outside of the building, thus proclaiming it to be 'arbour eights otel'. BOAC (British Overseas Airways Corporation) also used the hotel to house passengers and crews of the flying boats operating from the base at Poole Harbour Yacht Club (Salterns Marina). For further information on this, see the author's previous book 'Looking Back at Lilliput' published in 1999.

At the end of the war improvements were made to the hotel by the new owners, Mr & Mrs N A T McLeod, and was re-opened to the public in October 1947. It was acquired in the late 1950s by a company under the chairmanship of a Mr Fred Barnes, when the Directors were R M Smith, D G Harrocks, A Bell, and the manager was M. P Egli from Switzerland. An account dated October 1961 shows that a week's stay for two people cost £27.19s 5d (£27.95p) which included a 10% service charge.

Entrance to Harbour Heights Hotel December 2000 - Author's Collection

A four-page supplement with the Bournemouth Echo in October 1968 reported that since they bought the hotel in 1963 the owners Mr & Mrs T D Davies and Mr T E Webb have constantly made improvements; the transformation work which began in 1967 included an impressive new entrance with armour-plate glass costing £1500, twelve new en-suite rooms, two new cocktail bars, an extension to the restaurant to seat 140 diners and an improved 100 foot modern south facing sun terrace overlooking the Harbour.

Harbour Heights Hotel December 2000
Author's Collection

The manager at that time was Bournemouth born Mr John Knight, whose experience in the hotel trade included a number of years at the Palace Court Hotel (now the Bournemouth Hilton) in Westover Road under the then general manager, Gian Ronco, who will be remembered by many local people. The facilities available then at the Harbour Heights Hotel included provision for dinner dances (a new dance floor having been installed), weddings, private parties, buffet dances and in fact functions of any kind.

After fourteen years the Davies family sold the hotel to Mr Sam Hooper, a Glasgow businessman, whose ownership only ran for two years before he sold, in 1979, to Burden Hotels Limited, a family business consisting of Mr & Mrs Anthony Burden, their daughter Judy and son-in-law Paul Shee. The Burden family were well known Bournemouth hoteliers, having run two establishments on the West Cliff - the Mansfield and the Durley Grange for a considerable amount of time.

A number of extensions have improved the hotel over the years; it has five floors including the basement, and the Burden family added the top floor in 1984 producing another 15 bedrooms. One of the extensions was easy to spot as the floor in the corridor changed from wood to concrete.

When the very popular lunch time trade was initiated by them in 1980 there were very few local venues with similar facilities, the idea of offering simple straight-forward food as steak and kidney pie, curries and salads at reasonable prices filled a gap in the market - queues often formed as early as 12 o'clock as people tried to claim a window seat.

Due to diminished demand for its facilities the doors of the Harbour Heights Hotel were firmly closed two days before Christmas 2000 after serving the public for around 80 years. On passing the armour-plate glass entrance in the New Year of 2001, the last Christmas tree could still be seen inside standing dark and forlorn. Nevertheless, it was re-opened on Good Friday 2001 by the FJB Group, owners of the Sandbanks and Haven Hotels.

Part of the original 'Harbour Heights Estate', the apartment block 'The Conning Towers', situated in Haven Road (once West Road), is typical of the classic buildings of the 1930s - for the first time glass, reinforced concrete and tubular steel were used and formed the basis of new architectural designs and styles. The August 1936 issue of 'The Architect and Building News' gave a five page report on the property, which was constructed in 1934 as a private residence lavishly spread out through three spacious floors. 'The accommodation includes two features of special interest. One of these is the private cinema for amateur equipment, a fully equipped projection room with microphone and gramophone turntable for music and sound effects. The proscenium has footlights and electrically operated curtain. Another interesting feature is the large cantilevered sun lounge with continuous semicircular window, giving a fine view of the harbour. The circular column contains built-in loud speakers, operated from the principal receiving set in the living room. Of the five bedrooms, three have private balconies, with sliding and folding windows'.

Sam Goodman is listed as the occupant in 1939, under the heading of West Road and by 1961 and 1975, now under Haven Road, the property was owned by the Wellcome Foundation and is believed to have been a convalescent home for executives from that organisation.

Conversion work began in 1997 to transform The Conning Towers into a luxury art deco flat development, and in 1999 won that year's Poole Pride of Place Award for the sensitive restoration in art deco style. It also won for Poole a commendation in national environmental design, being one of 55 recognitions in the national Civic Trust Awards. Handled by Andrew Key estate agents, the architect was David Quigley from London, and EBC Construction the builders, from Poole.

The Conning Towers is a listed building, and now contains nine apartments and penthouses.

The Conning Towers
Courtesy: Andrew Key

CHAPTER ELEVEN
HAVENHURST HOTEL – CHADDESLEY GLEN – LITTLE FOSTERS

In close proximity to the Harbour Heights Hotel, a small block of six apartments now stands on the site of the old Havenhurst Hotel at the top of Chaddesley Glen. In the 1940s and 1950s the property was owned by a Colonel Curtis who ran it as a gentlemen's club or private drinking club, and there is a suggestion that there was a gaming house either at the Harbour Heights or the Havenhurst. It seems that at the end of the 1950s Colonel Curtis had wanted to sell out to a developer, but Mr & Mrs W. Palmer bought it in 1960 and ran a most successful establishment for fourteen years.

Havenhurst Hotel
Courtesy: Mr Lewis Shaw

A native of Wimborne Mr Palmer remembers as a child, between 1914 and 1920, accompanying his grandfather, who ran Hackney Carriages in the area, to Wimborne Station where he met the London trains and took passengers out to all the large estates including Kingston Lacy. Travelling in a horse drawn carriage over the gravel roads was not particularly comfortable, and at night the only illumination was the candles in the lanterns on the carriage. Around 1910 Mr Palmer's grandfather conveyed members of the Kaiser's shooting party to Kingston Lacy. Mr Palmer also remembers his grandfather's first motor car, a splendid landau type De Dion Bouton with huge headlamps.

After a career in the Scientific Civil Service, Mr Palmer chose to go into the hotel trade and so bought the Havenhurst Hotel, with financial help from a member of the Church of the

Transfiguration who wanted to conserve the property. During the first few years of the 1960s the Palmer family extensively refurbished the interior, extended the rooms to seventeen, each with private bathrooms, and installed central heating; the Havenhurst Hotel became a venue for local cocktail parties as well as attracting many visitors to Canford Cliffs.

Before reluctantly putting the hotel up for sale prior to 1974, due to ill-health, Mr and Mrs Palmer had wanted to buy another establishment, the Branksome Court Hotel in Haven Road opposite Canford Cliffs Library, for the sum of £60,000 but negotiations took so long they opted out. Mr Palmer continues to live in Canford Cliffs and has many happy memories of his ownership of the Havenhurst Hotel.

Believed to have been built in 1887, the Indenture of Conveyance for the Havenhurst was dated 20th July 1889 between the Reverend Hugh Pearson and Henry Fitzjames Barnes. A legal document of 16th June 1923 mentions Gwendoline Seale Gordon, John Lewis Randolph Gordon, Violet Marion Undine Lewis and Charles St John Kellet Roche.

The house 'A Choice Marine Residential Property with super sea views' was for sale in 1930 and from the estate agents particulars we learn that it stood in *'quiet secluded grounds, amidst pine trees, and commanded magnificent views'*. Together with three reception rooms, nine bedrooms (all with a fireplace), two bathrooms and compact, easily worked offices, was an excellent garage for two cars, chauffeur's cottage and useful outbuildings, and an acre of *'lovely garden with tennis court and picturesque woodland'*.

Precise details of its location tell us that it was situated in *'Chaddesley Glen, in the civil parish of Poole in the County of Dorset, on the borders of Hants, about 3½ miles from the centre of the progressively residential town of Bournemouth, which is connected by a 15 minute bus service running only a minute's walk from the property and also connecting Poole, Swanage and other places of interest. There is a splendid express train service between London and Bournemouth'*. We also learn that the church is five minutes walk, Post Office, Telegraph Office and shops ten minutes walk; a pillar box was to be found outside the property. Among the delightful amenities quoted are the nearby bathing beaches, golf courses and yachting facilities as well as *'good fishing in the harbour and sea'*.

The exterior was described as of a very substantial brick structure, rough cast and half-timbered, a tiled roof with partly creeper clad gables; standing in an elevated position on a wooded slope well back from a private road and sufficiently distant from the main road to avoid traffic nuisances.

The garage contained an inspection pit, there was a three roomed chauffeur's cottage and a harness room with fireplace, two stalls and a loose box. The garden had a full size tennis court and contained a shrubbery, rose covered pergola, small kitchen garden with fruit trees and a *'picturesque piece of woodland'*. The telephone number then was Canford Cliffs 23.

In 1974 the Havenhurst Hotel was for sale by auction with the benefit of Outline Planning Permission for redevelopment into flats. It was sold prior to auction within the price guide of £125,000 to £150,000 and, shortly after, the flats were developed by a local builder.

Part of the original garden wall can still be seen on the south side.

Havenhurst Hotel 1960s
Courtesy: Mr W. Palmer

That part of Chaddesley Glen from Haven Road (West Hill or West Road) to the corner was, up to 1939, designated as Church Road; it continued down past the Church of the Transfiguration and that section is now a footpath. The only property listed is Harbour Court apartments on the west side, which formed part of the Harbour Heights Estate. The lower part of Chaddesley Glen in 1918 contained four residences - Darenth, Endcliff, Chaddesley and Wykeham Lodge where lived The Reverend Gerald Egerton Boyle MA, priest in charge of the Chapel of the Transfiguration, and the wooden building of the first church.

This number had risen to 18 in 1939 with Reverend Boyle still at Wykeham Lodge, and by 1961 there were 32 properties listed including Little Fosters and the Havenhurst Hotel; Chaddesley House had been converted into flats. In 1975 Wykeham Lodge and Corfu had been demolished to make way for flats, The Reverend John V Rees is now Vicar of the Church of the Transfiguration and Hive Gardens is included in the Kelly's listing under Chaddesley Glen. The road was still unmade in the early 1970s.

On the cliff top at Chaddesley Glen are now two blocks of luxury apartments known as Little Fosters, situated on a three acre site where once stood a large mock-Tudor bungalow. During the 1950s it was owned by Sir Bernard and Lady Docker; he was a wealthy industrialist and his wife was described as a socialite with a flamboyant lifestyle, which was in stark contrast to the post-war austerity of the early 1950s. They drove around in a gold-plated Daimler, cruised the Mediterranean in their yacht *'Shemara'*, and their lavish parties were legendary. With various properties in Bournemouth and Poole, the Dockers often attended social events at Poole Harbour Yacht Club (Salterns Hotel) and moored their yacht off Brownsea Island. They later moved to Jersey and then Majorca - Sir Bernard died in 1978 in a Branksome Park nursing home and Norah, Lady Docker five years later in London.

In its 50 year history Little Fosters was home to Sir Bernard and Lady Docker for a relatively short time; built 1936/7 by Mr Charles W Bloomfield, it was demolished in 1989 and the site remained empty for several years before Harrison Developments received planning permission to erect two wings containing 20 apartments in the mid 1990s.

Mr C W Bloomfield was a Director of the London based Callender Cable Company and he and his wife Vera lived in Surrey before moving to Poole. The cliff top bungalow contained oak panelling, mullion stone fireplaces and sculpted solid oak doors with 'real' mortice and tenon joints. The peg roof tiles reputedly came from a monastery in the north of England and the lead scrolled gutters skirting the eaves were of a most elegant design. The grounds featured a magnificent water garden with a lake and a stream, and a waterfall constructed of Cumberland stone; a train was apparently specifically commissioned to transport the load of stone to a local railway station. Inside the property some of the ceilings were believed to have been copies of those at Hampton Court and the hall, which had a sprung floor, contained a gallery. In the days of the 1930s, life was much more formal and people dressed for dinner every night.

Little Fosters waiting to be demolished.
Author's Collection

The property was sold to Sir Bernard and Lady Docker during the 1950s and then when they themselves moved elsewhere, the original owners bought it back from them. Mr and Mrs Bloomfield owned a considerable amount of land and property in Chaddesley Glen and endeavoured to retain the pleasant atmosphere of the area whenever they sold a plot. The original house *'Corfu'* on the opposite corner to Little Fosters was purchased by a gentleman who indicated that under no circumstances would he sell to developers, but within a very short time his family had moved out and the property was demolished almost overnight without any prior warning. Mr and Mrs Bloomfield were not well pleased, and the apartments which now stand were the first to be built in Chaddesley Glen.

After Mr Bloomfield died, his wife continued to live at Little Fosters with her sister, and then moved to a smaller residence in Petersfield. The property remained empty and forlorn for sometime and gradually deteriorated into a poor state of repair, before being sold to a developer Mr Lionel Green, who at that time was owner of Compton Acres Gardens. Planning permission was granted for two blocks of 40 retirement homes with the bungalow being retained for communal facilities; Pamlion Properties - Mr Green's Company - did not go ahead and a few months later put in a further application to build two 4-storey blocks of flats and split the bungalow into three homes. Permission was not forthcoming and the site was then sold to Aria Estates from Ferndown, who wanted to erect 44 luxury retirement flats after demolishing the bungalow; this scheme was also turned down. Efforts were made to retain Little Fosters and the Borough of Poole tried to have it protected but the Department of the Environment decided it was not of sufficient historical value to become a listed building.

Many local folk will remember the beautiful grounds surrounding Little Fosters, as each year on a Wednesday in June Mr and Mrs Bloomfield were hosts to the Garden Party of the Church of the Transfiguration.

In the mid-1990s Harrison Developments bought the cliff top site and built the two wings providing 14 apartments and four penthouses.

Little Fosters 1988
Author's Collection

CHAPTER TWELVE
CHINES - PROMENADE - SIMPSON'S FOLLY

Canford Cliffs Chine before building of promenade c 1930
Courtesy: Mr David Morris

In July 1989 the Borough of Poole designated a small part of Canford Cliffs as a Conservation Area; this covers the whole of the Chine, Meriden Close, part of the Esplanade, The Circle and a small section of Cliff Drive. Their leaflet describes it as *'an area characterised by heavily wooded open space, giving an impression of spaciousness and tranquillity. Breaks of light and glimpses of the sea can be seen through the trees which contributes to the sylvan character of the locality'.*

Two distinct parts form the Conservation Area - The Chines and the houses surrounding them. *'The Chines form natural passages down to the sea, lined on either side by trees and shrubs providing a haven for wildlife. Towards the base of Canford Cliffs Chine is an informal grouping of 38 wooden beach huts arranged in a random fashion. The huts were built in the mid-1920s and form an attractive backdrop to the beach'.*

'Large, two-storey houses of red brick, render and clay tiled roofs, set in large grounds, situated around the top of the cliffs, create an attractive enclosure. The buildings date from the late Victorian and inter-war periods. They possess some attractive details such as corner turrets and ornate porches. The gardens are maturely landscaped, partly screening the buildings from the road'.

Under the heading of Preservation and Enhancement, aims are to maintain the pedestrian routes through the Chines, to retain the open space and mature landscaping, and any proposals for development on surrounding sites to be considered for the impact upon the setting of the Conservation Area.

Canford Cliffs Chine has in the past been referred to as Bitman's or Billman's Chine, Sugar Loaf Chine and Smugglers Chine, and Flaghead by the name of Beacon Chine - a mid 1760s map by Isaac Taylor shows a beacon or observation post symbol there.

When Dick Hartley's family came to Canford Cliffs in 1926, no promenade existed and they had one of the white beach huts in the Chine - number 21; he has a photograph of himself eating a jam sandwich outside the hut in July 1927. Other beach huts were temporary structures on the actual beach and were brought up in the autumn and put back in the spring; horses were used to haul them up the steep incline of the Chine before a flat bed lorry came into use. Sometimes these huts were swept away by the September gales. The beach in those days was much smaller than it is now and high tides brought the sea right up to the entrance of the Chine; before the promenade was built, the cliff was eroding at an alarming rate and Dick Hartley remembers a number of cliff falls and the disappearance of a cliff path.

In 1992 controversy arose with regard to the 1920s beach huts in the Chine; many of them had been allowed to fall into disrepair because the Council had planned to remove them, but a successful campaign was launched and a number of the huts were allowed to remain.

Canford Cliffs looking east - Beach Huts and Canford Cliffs Hotel
Courtesy: Mr David Morris
c 1930

The owner of the Canford Cliffs Hotel built a *'Martello Tower'* on the top of the Chine for his own use as a smoking room, the design imitated a Martello Invasion Fort. Andrew Hawkes has, in his collection of old postcards, one showing this structure with steps winding their way up from the bottom of the Chine. After a few years it became a casualty of cliff erosion and ended up on the beach as a pile of rubble.

Mr Ronald Pratt remembers the building of the sea wall and the zig-zag path down to the beach from Cliff Drive in the early 1930s; chutes were built to a First Level where a site hut and tables were positioned, and a night watchman installed, complete with brazier. Steel rods for reinforcement of the concrete were delivered by Foden Steam Wagons, and these and other materials were passed down the chutes; reinforcement frames were constructed on the tables and conveyed via a second chute down to the beach, and a steam hammer was used to drive in steel shutters for the retaining walls. As a young lad, Ronald Pratt was fascinated by all of this activity and he recalls that around this time a man committed suicide in the sea. The arrival of a police car or ambulance in Canford Cliffs would have attracted much attention, and he remembers seeing the stretcher with the body, brought up Flaghead Chine, complete with bowler hat perched on top.

Until the early 1960s, when it was blown up in order to complete the building of the promenade, Simpson's Folly provided a focal point on the beach between Flaghead Chine and Shore Road; the remains of a concrete house erected in the early 1880s gave amusement to children of all ages for many years. The property was one of the first to be constructed of concrete and Captain Simpson built his house as near as possible to the sea; unfortunately after only five days in residence a southerly gale sprang up and washed out the foundations, leaving the building unsafe. Simpson's Folly was blown up in 1890 by Poole Corporation workmen using 108 pounds of gunpowder and the resulting pile of rubble provided an ideal playground for generations of children. It had been hoped to preserve the Folly as an historical monument but this was not feasible and the promenade now covers the site on which it once stood.

Shore Road promenade, in 1985, was the setting for a fight between two rival ice cream operators for the BBC television series 'The Collectors'; the action involved one van ramming the other, after which a fight broke out between the two drivers. So realistic was the filming that a local resident dialled 999 to report that a road traffic accident had occurred between two ice cream vans on the promenade.

In Cecil N Cullingford's 'History of Poole' published in 1988, he quotes a paragraph from his grandfather's holiday journal of the early 1890s, when he journeyed by train from Clapham Junction to Bournemouth East (four hours and 25 minutes travelling time) and then walked *'along the beach to Durley Chine and past Canford Chine (broken sea-wall, all in ruins) and had refreshment at the Flagstaff Cottage, kept by Miss Eliza Jane Ridout (bread, ham, cheese and six large glasses of milk - total cost one shilling); smugglers once lived here. Near the Haven Hotel picked up a pipe-fish - numerous sand-hills, and razor fishes six inches long. Walked to Parkstone-on-Sea, passed the Beehive Inn and Model Farm Dairy, which we thoroughly inspected. Thence by the new road, close to the harbour, under the Railway Arch, thro' the People's Park (laid out by the Corporation - land given by Lord Wimborne)'.*

Simpson's Folly.
Courtesy: Mr John Trim

CHAPTER THIRTEEN
CHURCH OF THE TRANSFIGURATION

Reverend G E Boyle	1914-1940	Priest-in-Charge
Reverend Horace Coles	1941-1942	Priest-in-Charge
Reverend R Sherley-Price	1943-1952	Priest-in-Charge
Reverend John V H Rees	1952-1985	First Incumbent from 1956
Reverend Canon Rex Howe	1985-1994	
Reverend Jeremy Oakes	1995-	

A footpath leads up to Chaddesley Glen from the shore where the Church of the Transfiguration is to be found. Known to many as 'The Church in the Glen', its original official title was the Chapel of the Transfiguration; serving the parishes of Canford Cliffs and Sandbanks the first church building was of timber construction with a corrugated iron roof and was dedicated, as a daughter church of St Peter's in Ashley Cross, Parkstone, on 13th December 1911 by Bishop Ridgeway of Salisbury. Just over 50 years later it was re-built, increasing the seating capacity from 160 to 300, and consecrated by The Right Reverend The Lord Bishop of Salisbury on 26th May 1965, the Eve of the Feast of the Ascension. A joiner, Mr Brian Joiner, who had worked on the re-building of the Church since 1962, set the last pew front in position on the morning of the Consecration.

'Proposed New Church at Canford Cliffs' is the heading in The Parkstone Reminder of 7th November 1908. *'A meeting, by the kind permission and hospitality of Miss Rudd and Mademoiselle Asser, was held at the Redmoor School, Canford Cliffs, on Thursday afternoon 29th October, to consider the proposal to provide a Church in that district, which has considerably developed of late years, and for which The Reverend Hugh Pearson has generously offered an acre of land on the Chaddesley Estate.'* The Bishop of the Diocese presided, and was supported by the Archdeacon of Dorset, the Rural Dean, the Vicar, the Reverend Canon Bullock-Webster, C M Gane, J A Mackonochie, C G Doyne, A R Fernsby, G A D Beckingsale, Herbert Price and R L Kingsford.

Church of the Transfiguration c 1912
Courtesy: Mr Lewis Shaw

In his opening remarks The Bishop recalled that since he became head of the diocese 23 years ago, there had been a considerable growth in the population and Poole was known to be the largest borough in the diocese. They had to think of the future and with a mild climate, a nice seashore and fairly beautiful surroundings there was almost certain to be a further increase in the population.

The Vicar, Canon Dugmore, also mentioned the growth of the district which had occurred in his 36 years association with Parkstone, which had prompted the two separate parishes of All Saints and St Lukes. He expressed approval of the proposed new church at Canford Cliffs and spoke of the very useful purpose served for the Salterns area (Lilliput) by the Chapel of the Holy Angels built in 1874; it had been enlarged three times and was still frequently full to overflowing. At the same time it was pointed out that this place of worship was inaccessible to the large majority of persons resident at Canford Cliffs and Sandbanks. Further comment was made regarding the certain development of the land along the seashore, together with the fact that there was a piece of land held by the Diocesan Board of Finance at Northaven (sic) intended for the erection of a place of worship. *'It was felt that in days to come there would be a real town making up a charming resort in the district'.*

At the end of this initial meeting it had been resolved that they *'welcomed the proposed scheme to provide a Church to meet the growing needs of Canford Cliffs and the Sandbanks, and expressed its grateful thanks to the Reverend H Pearson for the generous gift of a suitable site for a Church and parsonage house'.* It was agreed that the Committee, out of which an executive would be formed would consist of Canon Dugmore (Vicar), the Rural Dean, Canon Inman, Canon Bullock-Webster, The Reverend C M Gane, The Reverend R L Kingsford, Dr Stafford, the Churchwardens of St Peter's, Messrs G J Piercy, A Fellowes, J E Appleton, W Johnson, E W Garthwaite and J L Bewsey.

Time was not wasted at this stage for the first meeting of the Committee was held on 14th November 1908 at the Parsonage House, Lilliput; additional names now appeared - Parish Chairman W Okes, and on the general committee Mr Sheriff Kentish, Mr Morgan, Colonel Nind and Mr Leonard Browne. It was proposed that the architect Mr Temple Morris be approached with regard to the proposed building and that an account be opened at the Canford Cliffs branch of the Wiltshire & Dorset Bank. It seems that the title of the church might have been St Dunstan, for this was the alternative name suggested by one of the committee members.

Minutes of meetings over the next few years indicate that the Committee did not readily accept that the land given by Reverend Hugh Pearson, who died before the church was built, was in a suitable position. They cast around for other sites and in particular, took an interest in plots on the 'Compton Acre Estate'. However, the Wimborne Estate solicitors wrote that their clients, owners of adjacent plots, before giving their consent required an Agreement should be made that no bell would be used in connection with the proposed church. The Committee felt that a guarantee of this kind could not legally be given, and wrote to Lady Wimborne asking her, as she had the power to so do, to over-ride the objections from the other plot owners.

Church of the Transfiguration c 1950
Courtesy: Miss Annette Bailey

Meanwhile, a meeting on 22nd February 1911 had to be hastily convened as letters had been received from the late Reverend Pearson's solicitors and from the Ecclesiastical Commissioners with reference to the Conveyance of the land. The solicitors sought to inform them that the site could only be used for the erection of a church or vicarage, and a further letter from one of Rev Pearson's executors stated that unless the Ecclesiastical Commissioners took over the land by 25th February, it would be offered at auction on 1st March. Questions also arose regarding maintenance of the roads adjoining the site until they could be handed over to the local authorities - those mentioned were Upper, Lower and South Chaddesley. They had been advised by the Town Clerk that church buildings are exempt from maintenance of the roads, and it was decided that only a church would be built, not a vicarage as this cleared up the problem of the roads.

It was decided that if they continued to reject the land given by the late Reverend Hugh Pearson, they might end up with no site at all, and it was resolved that a temporary church would initially be built with the thought that in due time, as more funds allowed, a permanent church would be erected. (It took 50 years).

Although a sum of £2000.00 had been suggested for the building of the new church, money did not seem to flow readily into the bank account. A suggestion by one of the Committee members that a box be placed in the Chapel of the Holy Angels to receive contributions, was later withdrawn. Various sums had been promised but in April 1911 the account only held £338.00. It seems that finance came from many small individual sums rather than any large donations.

Later Committee meetings in 1911 mentioned approval of the design for the temporary church submitted by Messrs Boulton & Paul from Norwich, and that Mr Herbert Kendall, an architect from Poole, would supervise all of the work in progress; rush seats were deemed to be preferable to any other and a book box rather than a bookshelf. The Committee were still meeting in March 1912 (after the building had been dedicated) and one item that had to be discussed was a letter from Mr Temple Morris, who was the architect chosen for the original, more permanent church. Since this was not erected and his plans not used, he was asking for payment with reference to the expenses he had incurred.

Wykeham Lodge in Chaddesley Glen (now flats) was the vicarage for a considerable number of years, and the first Priest-in-Charge was Reverend Gerald Egerton Boyle MA. Appointed in 1914 he remained until July 1940 when ill-health forced him to retire. In October that year Reverend Horace Coles succeeded him, but unfortunately his parishioners hardly had a chance to become acquainted - on a voyage to South Africa in November 1942, he lost his life when the ship in which he was sailing was sunk by enemy action (WWII 1939-1945).

On 1st January 1943, Reverend R Sherley-Price began his ministry and, as a result of his endeavours, Canford Cliffs and Sandbanks was made a Conventional District in 1945. The parish is part of the Deanery of Poole and the Archbishop of Dorset within the Diocese of Salisbury.

The Reverend John Vander Horst Rees was inducted as Priest-in-Charge on 29th June 1952 by Bishop Anderson of Salisbury, with the task of building a permanent Parish Church. In four years he had raised sufficient funds to establish an Endowment, thus enabling the formation of a Statutory District, and the Bishop appointed and licenced him as the first Incumbent in 1956.

During his 42 years of ministry Jack Rees, as he was habitually known, was a familiar figure in the area and would visit the various yacht clubs and local hotels, thus enabling him to make contact with people who did not necessarily attend church. He hailed from Bristol and had been the Organising Secretary for the Mission to Seamen, in which he continued to take an interest.

Mr J Rees, son of the Reverend J V H Rees, compiled a detailed record 'The Design and Construction of the Church of the Transfiguration, Canford Cliffs' and the author is grateful for his permission to now use this information.

The total cost of the re-building was £59,050.00 which included the church room and furnishings, the church with the tower and bells, pews in the nave and aisle, organ, church furnishings and the church garden. Before and during the re-building money was raised by an annual Gift Day and Fête and by covenanted subscriptions together with many smaller functions and individual donations. The whole project was based on local effort and all the contractors and companies involved were from Bournemouth and Poole, with the exception of the builders of the organ, who came from Taunton; the original instrument was from St Mary's on Brownsea Island.

It is interesting that in the early days of planning for the new church, the Parochial Church Council (PCC) gave thought to a fresh site, perhaps one closer to Canford Cliffs village itself, but as with the original Committee in the early 1900s, the decision was made to use land already in the possession of the church.

In the mid-1950s Lionel E Gregory, a local architect, was asked to submit plans for a new church. His first design was for a brick type building which resembled a miniature Coventry Cathedral. This was rejected for two reasons - it was felt that the design was ultra modern and not in keeping with the locality, and its position in the centre of the existing site would have resulted in the destruction of the unique and natural garden.

The architect then put forward the idea that the new building should be built around the original structure; the PCC agreed to this proposal, particularly as worship could continue throughout the reconstruction programme.

The tower was erected in 1957 since it had been decided that this would be a permanent structure and would form part of the new church building. On All Saints' Day that year the tower and nine bells were dedicated by the Venerable Malcolm Parr BA, Archdeacon of Warwick - the bells were the gift of relatives in memory of Major Eric John Roderick Brotherton MC, 2nd Battalion The Royal Tank Regiment who died in September 1944 (WWII) on Active Service in Italy. The bells - an octave and a 'calling bell' - are operated by a clavier, the largest weighing 12.5cwt and the smallest 3.5cwt. They are named after St Paul's 'Fruit of the Spirit' (Galatians V. 22 and 23) - Love, Joy, Peace, Long-Suffering, Gentleness, Goodness, Faith, Meekness, Temperance.

Before the building of the new church would begin, there was a more pressing need - that of a church room for Sunday School and other parochial activities. This was erected in 1960 at a cost of £3,500.00; designed by Lionel Gregory, the outside was finished in 'Snail Creep' pattern of Purbeck stone and the roof covered in copper ply felt. With toilet and kitchen facilities, the church room was placed in the north-eastern end of the existing structure so that it would easily be connected to the new church. This room was a pilot design and had the advantage of showing parishioners the outline of the forthcoming new building.

The Church of the Transfiguration

The Shield

A model of both the new church and the church room was made by a parishioner and was on display at the Garden Fête in June 1960. At frequent intervals during the afternoon a loud speaker from inside the model played a recording of the church bells, followed by organ music, and the Vicar's voice appealing for funds, with the following message: *'This charming model of our church and church room gives us an impression of how these will appear when the development scheme is completed. The architect's design, while increasing the size of the church and transforming it into a permanent structure, preserves its present charming character and natural surroundings. The population of the parish is increasing year by year and the need for extra accommodation is likely to become a matter of urgency in the near future. Even now we are frequently unable to accommodate the congregation on Festivals, and last Easter Day more than 60 people had to be turned away from Morning Service. But we shall only be able to achieve our object when we have the interest and support of every parishioner. Two other parishes in the Deanery of Poole, namely Hamworthy and Oakdale, have recently built beautiful Parish Curches, surely we, who are privileged to live in this most delightful place, are also ready to strive with all our might to build a beautiful permanent Parish Church to God's Glory in Canford Cliffs. This great task is a challenge to one and all of us. Are you playing your part?'* This appeal by the Vicar did much to further the re-building finances.

Work actually started on the re-building programme in November 1962. Before this date, however, there was much thought and discussion with regard to which end of the new church should be started first. The major problem was that of money; at that stage the amount of finance available seemed to indicate that it would be sensible to begin on the West end as opposed to the East end, which was likely to cost the greater amount of money. Many members of the PCC considered it essential to start on the West end since this could easily be seen from the road and passers-by would be more likely to be aware of the work in progress. Both the Vicar and the Architect understood this point of view, but were themselves convinced that commencement should be at the East end since this was, after all, the working part of the church. They felt sure that once construction began, people would realise the potential beauty of the building and subscribe generously. Agreement was reached with the PCC that work should start at the East end, and the contractors were commissioned, and indeed before the workmen moved in, sufficient funds were available to cover the complete development of the East end.

The Sanctuary, Chancel, Vestries, Sacristy and boiler room are all part of the East end, and the design of The Sanctuary was governed by the Apse, which is half-moon in shape and stands directly behind the Altar. The Vicar was keen to have the Apse incorporated into the new church for it was his experience that uncluttered Apses produced remarkably good acoustics, thus helping the congregation as well as reducing the strain on the Vicar's voice. The echo in the Church of the Transfiguration is rated at one second with the building empty and reduces according to the number in the congregation; the acoustics are, therefore, extremely good. Visiting organists are not always happy with this for it means that the slightest error is easily heard. This does not happen in a church with a substantial echo because the notes tend to 'run' together and a mistake is lost in the confusion of sound.

The re-building of the East end took eight months and all the Services continued to be held during that time; the Altar was moved to a central position at the head of the nave and the organ to the north-west end. The congregation adapted themselves to the unusual conditions, and more than one bride walked up a dust-sheeted aisle under a canopy of ivy-decorated scaffolding. The new Sanctuary and Chancel were used for the first time on the Sunday before Christmas 1962 and during that severe winter, which lasted until March 1963, sheets of industrial polythene separated worshippers from several feet of snow. Conversely, asphalt was laid during an unusual heat wave in the summer.

Whilst the West end was being built, the entrance to the church was through the lobby door next to the bell tower; it was not a very convenient arrangement but it did allow workmen to continue without interruptions.

Next to be constructed was the Galilee Porch - this was deemed to be a convenient meeting place for people before entering church, particularly in wet weather. It contains such useful items as umbrella stands and benches together with church literature, but is also an attractive area with terrazzo flooring and the two niches, with concealed lighting, are occupied by wrought iron symbols depicting The Crown of the Passion and The Crown of Glory.

One of the Choir Gates
Author's Collection

The half-moon shaped alcove in the north aisle is situated where the Sunday School children sit when they attend on the first Sunday of each month. Flowers are often displayed there but its reason for being, is that the Vicar, Jack Rees, wanted a place where he could show certain features of the church's year. The four occasions which attract most interest are The Crib at Christmas, Calvary Hill during Holy Week, the Easter Garden and the Advent Candles for the four Sundays during Advent. By putting small displays in the niche, it helps many worshippers, especially children, to appreciate the significance of church dates of particular note.

The Cross and Candle Sticks in the Lady Chapel came from the High Altar of the original church. This Chapel is most often used for occasional services when a limited number of worshippers attend, and the curtains allow it to be fully enclosed as a separate entity when required.

The black roof timbers of the original building were retained, as was the Chancel Arch and flooring; Japanese Oak and African Doussie wood were used for the Altar, choir stalls, pulpit, lectern and High Altar rails. The decoration on the choir stalls represents the four seasons in flowers and foliage - a sidesman, who was a gifted woodcarver, began work on the panels but died suddenly with the carvings unfinished and they were eventually completed by another craftsman.

Much of the woodwork, including the pews, was made in the workshop beneath the church - a great deal of research was carried out to ensure that the pews were as comfortable as possible for the majority of the congregation, as the Vicar held the opinion that uncomfortable conditions were not conducive to worship. The joiner was asked to make up an adjustable seat with regard to height and rake of the back, and twenty volunteers of various shapes and sizes came on duty. Watched by the Vicar, the architect and the joiner, the dimensions of the pews were then worked out. It must have been quite an interesting occasion.

The 'Snail Creep' Purbeck stone was used externally, and set within the North Pillar in The Sanctuary is the Consecration Stone which is of 'Purbeck Thornback' - a marble found only in narrow seams at considerable depth; the Credence Table on the south side of the Apse is of the same stone. On the three enamelled shields to the choir gates The Bible represents The Word of God; The Lamb represents The Son of God; The Dove represents The Holy Spirit; the Font at the entrance is from the original Church.

It was gratifying for all those concerned with the project that virtually everything inside the new church was given in memory of a loved one, or as a special thank offering. Although it was decided that plaques would not be appropriate, a book was compiled which contains all the relevant information. The painting of 'The Transfiguration' in the south aisle is a memorial to the Reverend Horace Coles, and 'The Crucifixion' in the north aisle, by a local artist, was inspired by Salvador Dali's 'Christ of St John of the Cross'.

The Church of the Transfiguration is full of natural light from the clear glass windows - the only stained glass is in the four Roundels on the Lady Chapel Screen, and two windows in the Vestry. The Roundels portray St Anne with the Blessed Virgin Mary as a girl; Mary with the baby Jesus; Joseph with the child Jesus, and Jesus blessing a little child - these depictions were created at the particular request of the Vicar. The two sections of glass in the vestry windows, although not having any ecclesiastical significance, are thought to be good examples of late 19th Century stained glasswork and were originally placed in the banqueting hall of Avon Castle. It was considered unwise to put them in direct contact with the elements and are hung between the plain glass in the vestry windows, thus giving privacy to the Vicar.

Above the Altar in the apse roof, natural light has been used to great advantage; cast into the concrete are thirty four glass lens units which tend to act as a bank of spot lights. The effect on the Altar area is impressive, particularly in the summer months when the sun is high; artificial light in the Chancel and Sanctuary is used during Services and this gives a 'sense of depth'. The focal point of the church is the Cross above the Altar which is silhouetted from a strip of light let into the back of the Cross. It is often switched on when the church is not being used for Services, this is for the benefit of visitors who, when they see it for the first time, are impressed to a point where they stand and gaze at the scene for several minutes.

The simplicity of the Cross against the plain wall of the Apse is indeed most effective and is due to the determination of the Vicar. Initially it was felt that the plain wall might need some embellishment - many ideas were put forward to overcome the featureless appearance ranging from paintings to a statue, but Jack Rees was not impressed with any of the suggestions. Once the Cross was in position people realised that the Vicar was right, and indeed many were convinced that the design of the Cross complemented the overall character of the church.

The comprehensive record of the building of the new church written by Mr J Rees, son of the Vicar, covers everything in great detail, and other chapters include Vestments and Furnishings, the Church Plate, Heating, Ventilation and Lighting, the Organ Specification, Bells and Clavier, a complete list of the contractors and the names of trees and shrubs. It is evident that each stage of the re-building was closely monitored by the Vicar and the architect, the craftsmen and the PCC in an endeavour to create a beautiful church for the Parish of Canford Cliffs and Sandbanks.

'The Cross' Author's Collection

'Millennium West Window' by Sally Scott
Courtesy: Mr Nick Carter

Construction was completed in 1964 and on Wednesday 26th May 1965 the Consecration Ceremony was conducted by the Right Reverend Joseph Fison, recently enthroned as the Bishop of Salisbury. The first service in the Consecrated church was Holy Communion at 08.00 the following day - The Feast of Ascension.

Later that year, A Service of Thanksgiving to celebrate the Bi-Centenary Year of the Lodge of Amity took place on 3rd October with Brother Reverend J V H Rees Presiding. *The Harvest Festival decorations enhanced the occasion as did the singing of the choir. The address was given by Worshipful Brother The Venerable David Rokeby Maddock, later Suffragen Bishop of Dulwich.* Another Service of Thanksgiving was held on 26th June 1977 to mark the 25th Anniversary of the Induction of the Reverend J V H Rees.

In 1985 Jack Rees retired at the age of 80, and was succeeded later in that year by Canon Rex A Howe MA(Cantab). Previously Dean of Hong Kong Cathedral, he became Team Rector and Rural Dean of Grantham in 1977 and four years later was appointed a Canon and Prebendary of Lincoln Cathedral. His Induction at the Church of the Transfiguration was on 4th September 1985, and in 1992 Canon Rex Howe became the Rural Dean of Poole following Canon Peter Huxham's move from St Peter's in Ashley Cross to become Chaplain at Taunton Hospital.

The present Incumbent, Reverend Jeremy Oakes came to Canford Cliffs in 1995, having previously been Team Vicar at St Paul's on Canford Heath - part of the Oakdale Team. He read Theology at Westcott College, Cambridge and his parishes have been in the Midlands, Gerrards

Cross, Putney in South West London and St John's at Poulner, near Ringwood. Reverend Jeremy Oakes is a Fellow of the Institute of Chartered Accountants of England & Wales, and is Chairman of the Salisbury Diocesan Board of Finance.

Funds raised by the parishioners for the Millennium Appeal were used to improve church facilities, including a disabled access, and a new west window especially engraved for the occasion. Created by Sally Scott, some of whose work can be seen in Westminster Abbey, 'The Transfiguration' window was dedicated by the Bishop of Basingstoke in January 2000.

The tiny church of St Nicolas was built in Panorama Road in 1929 as a chapel-of-ease for those parishioners who found it difficult to reach the Church of the Transfiguration (few people owned motor cars in those days). A wooden structure, it was built by A D Saunders of Longfleet Road, Poole, at a cost of £460.2s.0d (£460.10p).

As with the mother church, it was just over 50 years before a new building took its place - the old one suffered from woodworm and rot, and was very cold in winter. The re-building scheme was planned by the late Vicar, Reverend Jack Rees in 1980 with completion in 1983 —the whole development included two bungalows for retired clergy. The foundations for these were laid at the same time as the chapel was built and, as more money became available, they were completed in 1984 and 1985. The total cost was £98,000 and apart from a £5,000 gift from the Diocese and a £15,000 loan, the finances were raised by local people.

The bell, organ and triptych were salvaged from the original wooden building, and the new chapel was dedicated by the Right Reverend Bishop of Sherborne, the Right Reverend John Kirkham. The architect was Mr Eric Gregory and the builder, Mr Baron Levine.

Line drawing of Church of the Transfiguration   Courtesy: Miss Annette Bailey

The author wishes to thank Mr J Rees and Miss Annette Bailey for their considerable help with this chapter; also to the Reverend Jeremy Oakes for permission to use the church archives.

APPENDIX 'A'

CANFORD CLIFFS VILLAGE

1918

North Side

Rumsey & Rumsey - Auctioneers
Parade Tobacco Stores
Dean Mrs M.B. Post & Telegraph Office
Lowe Bros. Motor Engineers
Malmesbury & Parsons' Dairies Limited
Swift Alexander, Antique dealer
Ryall Ernest Alfred. Boot maker

South Side

Parsons George & Son, Dairymen and Cowkeepers
Voysey & Co. Confectioners
Holloway Frank, Auctioneer, Estate Agent & Valuer.
Canford Cliffs Motor Omnibuses (George Fox, proprietor)
Canford Cliffs & District Land Co. (Frank Holloway, Secretary)
Sandbanks Rail-less Electric Car Co. (Frank Holloway, Secretary)
Day Robert, Fruiterer
Hill Dudley George
Crouch W.T & Sons Cabinet Makers
Taylor Edwd.H. MPS Chemist
Greatorex & Crowe, Haberdashers
— *here is Maxwell Road* —

CANFORD CLIFFS VILLAGE

1939

North Side

19 Parish Miss N. Newsagent
19a Mann Miss Jane, Corsetiere
19b Rowe Allan
20 Mettem Jesse E.
20 The Canford Cliffs Motors Ltd
21 Motor Engineers
21 Cox Wm. Hy.
21b Loader Arth.
22 Canford Cliffs Fruit Stores
   (Channell & Channell)
22 Ellis Misses
23 Ames Edwd
23 Scott & Scott Ltd. Ironmongers
24 Knighton Geo. T. Butcher
24a Cousins & Co. Commission Agents
25 Thorne Frank
25 Thornes Garage
26 Nat Provincial Bank (J D Bond mngr)
26 Stacey Miss
27 Lloyds Bank Ltd.(L.E. Reece mngr)
27a Marchant Miss
28a Helene, Ladies Wear Specialist
29 Pierce Mrs Enid, Pastrycook
29 Witherington A&R. Hairdressers
29 Barrett R.B & Sons. Cars for Hire
30 Bunce Fredk.Jn. Boot Maker
30 Hillman H.J. Builder
31 & 32 Harrison's Fishmongers
33 Day Geo.S. Fruiterer
34 Mason Miss Vera.Ladies Hairdresser
35 Godsell Richard. Auctioneer & Est.Agent
35a Southern Cigar Co. Tobacconists
36 Alborno Albert. Cooked Meat Shop
37 Short S. Chemist
— *here is Elmstead Road* —

South Side

1 Palmer Chas. Ernest
1 Malmesbury & Parsons Dairies
1 Parsons P & Sons Ltd. Bakers
2 Hudson Bros. Ltd Grocers
2 Steel Fred
3 Voysey & Co. Baker
3 Pethen Frederick C. Motor Cars
   For Hire Tel. Canford Cliffs 253
3 Pethen Mrs F. Ladies Hairdresser
4 Rumsey & Rumsey FAI Estate
   Agents, Auctioneers, Surveyors &
   Valuers
4 The Canford Cliffs Land Society
   (Rumsey & Rumsey, Secretaries)
5 Pauline, Antiques
6 Model Farm Dairies(Bmth)Ltd.
6 Leith Clement
7 Crouch W.T.& Sons Cabinet mkrs
7 Wareham Bulb Growers Ltd
8 Pars & Co. Chemists
8 Forsey J.W.
9 Smith Mrs M.P. Draper
   — *here is Maxwell Road* -
10 Stimpson Jack Newsagent
11 International Tea Company
12 Telephone Exchange
12 Brine F.E. Tailor & Outfitter to
   Gentlemen & their sons
14 Hales Wltr. Tobacconist
15 Symons C H. Wine & Spirit Mch
16 Power R.H. Bookseller
17 'Topaz' Furnishings - G.Nicklen
18 Davis Mrs M. Cafè
   — *here is Cliff Drive* -

CANFORD CLIFFS VILLAGE

1961

North Side

    Canford Cliffs Motors - Petrol Station
19 Randles & Churcher - Tobacconists
19a Miss J. Mann - Corsetière
20 Canford Cliffs Motors Ltd.
22 Fox & Sons - Estate Agents
23 Canford Cliffs Hardware - Ironmongers
24 Dixon, Harry & Son - Butchers
25 Thorne's Garage - Motor Engineers
26 National Provincial Bank Ltd.
27 Lloyds Bank Ltd.
28 Home Bakery (Bournemouth) Ltd
28a Jervis F.E. - Wool Shop
28 (rear) Hillman H.J. & Co. - Builders
29 Bird Wm. H. - Ladies Hairdresser
30 Midland Bank Ltd
31 Harrison Chas. - Fishmonger & Poulterer
33 Torquils - Fruiterers & Florists
34 Laurence of Canford Cliffs - Ladies Hairdresser
35 Godsell. Richard - Estate Agent & Valuer
35 Southern Cigar Co. Ltd. - Tobacconists
36 Canford Cliffs Radio-Electro - Radio & TV
37 Short S. Chemist & Post Office
    — *here is Elmstead Road* —

South Side

1 Malmesbury & Parsons Dairies
2a W.A.G. Adams - Radio, T.V. and Electrical Engineers
2 Hudson Bros. Ltd. - Grocers
3 Naylor F.G. & C.L. - Gowns
4 Rumsey & Rumsey - Estate Agts
5 Eldridge Pope & Co - Wine Mrct
6 Merrill. Capt. C.
7 Haven Cleaners & Dyers.
8 Barnetson. Claude - Chemist
9 Seasales Ltd. Yachting Outfitters
    — *here is Maxwell Road* -
10 Randles & Churcher - Tobccnsts
11 International Tea Co. Store.
11 D'Angibau & Malim - Solicitors
12 Telephone Exchange
13 Hansford F.C. Gents Outfitters
14 Maxwells - Fruiterers
15 Castle & Co. Wines & Spirits
16 Galleon Bookshop
17 Pets & Gardens
18 St. Clair's Cafè
    — *here is Cliff Drive* —

CANFORD CLIFFS VILLAGE

1975

North Side

2-10 Canford Cliffs Motors Ltd
12   Fox & Sons - Estate Agents
12a Robson Cotterell Ltd
14   Canford Cliffs Hardware Stores
14a Jones. Frank & Co. Solicitors
16   Dixon. Harry & Son - Butchers
16a Janus Doors Ltd - Luxury Doors
16a Colley, Meikle & Co. Heating Engineers
20   National Westminster Bank Ltd.
22   Lloyds Bank Ltd.
22a F.C. Finance Ltd. - Hire Purchase
24   Wool Shop
26   Victoria Bakery
28   Dodarell Shelagh - Ladies Hairdresser
30   Midland Bank Limited
32   Harrison Chas. - Fishmonger & Poulterer
34   Tanner P.F. - Butcher
36   Gowns - Fashion Specialists
38   Berys - Fashion Shop
40   Southern Cigar Company
40a D'Angibau & Malim - Solicitors
42   Godsell. Richard - Estate Agent
44   Canford Cliffs Electro. - Radio Specialists
45   Short S. - Chemist & Post Office
— *here is Elmstead Road* —

South Side

1   Gillets - Grocers
3   Adams - Television Dealers
5   Carousel - Ladies Hairdresser
7   Iris - Gowns
9   Whittle L.M. Greengrocer
11 Rumsey & Rumsey - Estate Agts
11a Tomei, Mackley & Pound-Arcts.
13 Eldridge Pope & Co.-Wine Mrct
15 Barclays Bank Ltd.
19 Griffin F.E. - Chemist
21 Sea Sales - Yachting Outfitters
— *here is Maxwell Road* -
23 N.S.S. Newsagents
25 International Stores Ltd.
27 Telephone Exchange
29 Canford Manshop - Outfitters
31 Maxwells - Fruiterers
33 Wine Market - Wines & Spirits
35 Galleon Bookshop & Stationers
37 Pets & Gardens
39 St. Clair Restaurant
— *here is Cliff Drive* -

CANFORD CLIFFS VILLAGE

2001

North Side

Magna Motor Company Limited
Fox & Sons - Estate Agents
Ellis Jones - Solicitors
Henry's Wine Bar
Haven Flowers
Johnson - Dry Cleaning
National Westminster Bank Plc.
Lloyds Bank Plc.
Canford Aviation
Village Bakery
Canford Cliffs Pharmacy
H S B C Bank Plc.
Freeride Surf
Executive Homes - Estate Agents
Pizza Rapida
Berys - Ladies Fashions
D'Angibau Willmot - Solicitors
Elegance - Ladies Hairdressers
Haven Road News & Post Office
— *here is Elmstead Road* —

South Side

Berkeleys - Estate Agents
5 La Pince - Ladies Hairdresser
Iris - Ladies Fashions
Justins - Food Store
Atkins - Estate Agents
Canford Cliffs Associates
Le Chateau - Restaurant
Barclays Bank Plc.
Portman Building Society
Andrew Key & Drummond
   - Estate Agents
Rawlings - Electrical Contractor
— *here is Maxwell Road* —
J M E Store - Newsagents
Threshers - Wine Merchants
Telephone Exchange
Edward Jones Investments
Select World Travel
Pommes Frites - Restaurant
Vivette Interiors - Soft Furnishings
One to One Care
  - Mobility Specialists
Goadsby & Harding - Estate Agents
— *here is Cliff Drive* —

ACKNOWLEDGMENTS

I am grateful to the following for providing me with information, and thank them for their help. Please forgive me if I have forgotten anyone.

Mrs Jane Attia, Mr R F Adlem, Mrs H Baggaley, Miss Annette Bailey,
Mr Tony Baker, Miss H Beckwith, Mr J Biggs - Borough of Poole,
Mrs Pat Borley, Bournemouth Evening Echo, Mr H A Bowman FRICS,
Miss Helen Brotherton CBE., BT Archives, Canford Cliffs Land Society,
Canford Cliffs Library, Mrs Christine Clarke, Mrs Sheila Collins,
Mrs Jean Cooper, Mrs Nina Crane, Mr A R Crouch, Dorset Healthcare
NHS Trust, Mrs E Eaton, Mrs Enid Green, Mrs Eileen Greenhill,
Captain R E Hartley RN(Rtd), Mr Martin Hickson, Mr Roger Lees FRICS,
Mrs Mary Lobley, Mr W Palmer, Miss L Parkin MBE, Poole Local History Service,
Poole Reference Library, Mr Ronald Pratt, Mr J Rees, Miss Betty Savage,
Mr Paul Shee, Mr M Shutler, Mrs Sheila Thompson, Mrs Beryl Thomas,
Mr Gerry Wareham, Mrs DeniseWinton.

BIBLIOGRAPHY

Grant-Braham, Bruce	*The Collectors 1986*
Hawkes, Andrew	*Memories of Old Poole-Canford Cliffs 1986*
Pevsner, Nikolaus & Newman	*The Buildings of England 1972 - Dorset*
Poole Historical Trust	*An Album of Old Poole 1975*
Seymour, Mike & Balderson	*To the ends of the Earth - 210 Squadron's Catalina Years 1999*

INDEX

A

All Saints' Church, Branksome Park 8
Archer, Sir John KBE JP 12, 39
Arlott, Mr John 39
Avenue, The. Branksome Park 6

B

Baden-Powell, Lady Olave 42
Balmoral, Paddle Steamer 25
Barff, Reverend Canon A J 29
Beard, Mr J Stanley 47, 49
Bennett, Dr F G 20
Bloomfield, Mr C W 65
BOAC 17, 40
Bodley Scott, Mr T 4
Bonham-Christie, Mrs Florence 11
Brady, Mr John 50
Branksome Court Hotel 8
Brotherton, Miss Helen CBE 10, 11
Brownsea Island 11, 54
Bygraves, Mr Max 18, 19

C

Cartmel Private Hotel 20
Cassels, Sir Ernest 32
Chamberlain, Mr Neville 45
Chartcombe 51
Clark, Mr John 52
Cliff Café 8, 9
Cload, Mr Thomas 47
'Collectors, The' 50, 70
Cooper, Mr & Mrs Jimmy 17,18,19
Cornelia Hospital 44, 46
Cornish, Mr W V 9
Cosy Coaches 25
Crouch, Mr A 16

D

Darroch, The Misses 21
Dawn Trust 55

De Horsey, Admiral 11
De Ramsey, Baron 47
Dean, Mrs Becky 33
Docker, Sir Bernard & Lady 30, 65
Domesday Book 4
Dorset Corner House Hotel 11
Dorset Wildlife Trust 10, 11

E

Ebdon House Hotel 24
Eldridge Pope 13
Ellison, Lt Col G F 4
Eysoldt, Mrs 42-46
Eysoldt, Mr Charles 42-46

F

Fellows, Mrs Margaret neé Tucker 42-46
Fitz Club 4,11,19,33,34
Fitzgerald, The Hon Mrs E 34
Flaghead Chine 4,36,44
Foott, Miss/Mrs Dingwall 25
Forsyte Shades 26,52
Furzey Island 23

G

George, Mr William 13,14,49
Goathorn 56
Green, Mr Lionel 51
Gregory, Mr Lionel 76,77
Grey Rigg 42
Greystoke Hotel 29,53,54

H

Harbour Heights Estate 61,64
Harrison, Mr Charles 21,29,31,38,85,86
Harrison Developments 65,67
Hartley, Captain R E 17,24,68
Harvey Nicholls 42
Haven Hotel 26
Hawthorns Hotel 43
Haynes, Alderman A B 9,32
Hession, Reverend Brian 29

Hewitt, Mr E 12
Hillman, Mr H J 29,85,86
Holloway, Mr Frank 4,28,84
Holloway Sanatorium 57
Holton Heath 46
Holy Angels, Church of 50
Howe, Earl 47
Hutchings, Mr C R 4

I

Imperial Airways 40

J

James, Mr Sid 18
James & Sons 47
Jebb, Mr J J 4
Jebb, Mr G S W 4
Jones, Mrs Joyce, Mayor of Poole 9

K

Kemp-Welch, Mr S E 4
King Charles Inn 56

L

Langran, Dr Bartholomew 17,38
Langran, Mrs 44
Liddell, Mr Alvar 52
Llewellin, Miss Mary JP 50
Lyle, Sir Leonard MP 13,53,54

M

Malmesbury & Parsons 38,84,85,86
McLeod, Mr N A T 29,59
Medwin, Miss G 20
Milne-Redhead, Mr W E 12

N

'Night Jar', The 19
Norfolk Lodge Hotel 4,23,33,35,36
North, Mr D 34

O

Odlum, Dr Doris 39
Orton Rigg Hotel 39

P

Palace Court Hotel 60
Parkstone Golf Club 52
Parkstone Golf Course 46
Piercy Mr G J 4
Poole Harbour Yacht Club 52,59
Poole Maritime Trust 10
Pratt, Mr M 21
Pratt, Mr R 21,70

R

RAF 210 Squadron 40,59
Randall, Mr G 25,27
Rebbeck Bros 5,16
Rhodes, Mr Wilfred 39
Risk, Dr Robert S 20,45
Riviera Hotel 20
Rowe, Cllr Freddie 17
Round Island 23
Royal Albert Hall 45
Royal Blue Coach 44,45
Rudd, Edith 12,33
Rumsey & Rumsey 34,39,84-87

S

St Nicolas Chapel 83
Salterns Marina 50
Scott, Sally 81,83
Seal, Mr A J 17,58
Sea Witch Hotel 5,34,35
Shaftesbury, Lord 57
Shepherd, Mr Horace 52
Shore Road 44,58,59
Short, Mr B C 9
Simpson, Mr T W 26,47,49
Simpson's Folly 44
Styles, Dr W V T 20
Sunderland Flying Boat 40

T

Tanner's Pork Pies 31
Teasdale Hotel 33
Tennis Club 26
Titley, Mr S H 12
Transfiguration, Church of 24,29,59

U

Umney, Mr R - Sheriff of Poole 41

V

Vauxhall Bridge 41

W

WWI 27
WWII 17,21,24,31,34,38,40,45,47,49,54,59
Webb, Sir Thomas 47
Weld, Sir Joseph 39
Westover Ice Rink 44
Wilde, Dr R F 11
Wimborne, Baron 4,47
Wimborne Minster 55
Women's Institute 14,45
Woolf, Mr T 8